The
Yellow Nib

The Yellow Nib is the annual journal of the Seamus Heaney Centre for Poetry at Queen's University Belfast. The title of the journal is inspired by a bird-call – or rather, by how that call inspired an anonymous Irish scribe of the ninth century to write the verses you see in the margin of this page. The aim of *The Yellow Nib* is simple: to publish good writing.

Int én bec
ro léc feit
do rinn guip
glanbuidi

fo-ceird faíd
ós Loch Laíg,
lon do chraíb
charnbuidi

9th century Irish

The small bird
chirp-chirruped:
yellow neb,
a note-spurt.

Blackbird over
Lagan water.
Clumps of yellow
whin-burst!

Seamus Heaney

the little bird
that whistled shrill
from the nib of
its yellow bill:

a note let go
o'er Belfast Lough—
a blackbird from
a yellow whin

Ciaran Carson

GENERAL EDITOR

Ciaran Carson

ADDRESS FOR CORRESPONDENCE

The Seamus Heaney Centre for Poetry
School of English
Queen's University Belfast
Belfast BT7 1NN
Northern Ireland
phone: +44 (028) 9097 1070
e-mail: shc@qub.ac.uk
www.qub.ac.uk/heaneycentre

TRADE ORDERS AND DISTRIBUTION

Angela Mallon
Blackstaff Press
4c Heron Wharf
Sydenham Business Park
Belfast BT3 9LE
phone: +44 (028) 9045 5006
email: info@blackstaffpress.com
www.blackstaffpress.com

ISBN 0-85640-791-7

The
Yellow Nib

The Literary Journal of the
Seamus Heaney Centre for Poetry

VOLUME 2

2006

This volume published in 2006 by
Blackstaff Press
4c Heron Wharf, Sydenham Business Park
Belfast BT3 9LE
with the assistance of the Arts Council of Northern Ireland

Typeset by Carole Lynch, County Sligo, Ireland
Printed in England by Cromwell Press

A CIP catalogue record for this book
is available from the British Library

ISBN 0-85640-791-7

www.blackstaffpress.com

Contents

Editorial

The Bangor Blackbird
Anonymous, ninth century

Just audible over the waves
a blackbird among leaves
whistling to the bleak
lough from its whin beak.

DEREK MAHON

In his essay 'Blackbird' in the first issue of *The Yellow Nib*, John Wilson Foster commented that one can fancy the poem which gave the journal its title as 'mischievously welcoming versions of itself'. One could also suggest that the poem is itself a version, its elegant syllabic form an attempt to transcribe the gorgeously unintelligible but no doubt meaningful notes of the 'feathered songster'. It is probable that the poem was written in the margin of an ecclesiastical Latin text. For all we know, it might have been a comment on that text, a kind of gloss or translation; moreover, the syllabics which replaced the earlier stressed forms of Irish verse are thought to have been developed from Latin verse. The patterns of one language leave their traces on another. Circles of song intersect.

The blackbird poem inhabits a liminal space. This is where translation happens, and *The Yellow Nib* is concerned with that space, among others. The present issue contains translations of Rilke by a Scot, of Ingeborg Bachmann by an Irishwoman, and of the Roman dialect poet Giuseppe Giachino Belli by an Australian. Michael Foley's odes are playful spins on Catullus. Derek Mahon's three poems are translations of a kind, versions or adaptations. These varieties of English are bent in an interesting way by a combination of native resource and openness to other forms of expression: so the margin becomes the centre.

> When the blackbird flew out of sight
> It marked the edge
> Of one of many circles.

> Wallace Stevens, 'Thirteen Ways of Looking at a Blackbird'

CIARAN CARSON
JUNE 2006

Int én bec
ro léc feit
do rinn guip
    glanbuidi

fo-ceird faíd
ós Loch Laíg,
lon do chraíb
    charnbuidi

  9th century Irish

The small bird
chirp-chirruped:
yellow neb,
    a note-spurt.

Blackbird over
Lagan water.
Clumps of yellow
    whin-burst!

  Seamus Heaney

the little bird
that whistled shrill
from the nib of
    its yellow bill:

a note let go
o'er Belfast Lough—
a blackbird from
    a yellow whin

  Ciaran Carson

Five Poems

PAUL FARLEY

The Westbourne at Sloane Square

You again! Of all the bomb-scarred stonework
and air vents underfoot I knew by heart.
You, still going strong in your black pipe
above the passengers and mice-live tracks.
You, flowing through eighteenth-century parkscape
into an ironclad late Victorian night.

Pissed and standing on the eastbound platform
I was a tin soldier who'd fallen in
to London's storm drain, sent spinning around
the Circle Line long after closing time,
and all along I've carried these trapped sounds
I hear again and recognise deep down.

How many miles of shit have you crawled through
since we last met? I'd do it all again.
We've less choice than we think, the likes of you and me.
Blind water, borne along or bearing through,
escaping in a hurry for open sea.
To think we start as innocent as rain.

The Yellow Nib, Vol. 2, 2006, pp. 1–5
© Paul Farley

Johnny Thunders Said

You can't put your arms around a memory.
The skin you scuffed climbing the black railings
of school, the fingertips that learned to grip
the pen, the lips that took that first kiss
are gone, my friend. Nothing has stayed the same.
The brain? A stockpot full of fats and proteins
topped up over a fire stoked and tended
a few decades. Only the bones endure,
stilt-walking through a warm blizzard of flesh,
making sure the whole thing hangs together,
our lifetimes clinging on as snow will lag
bare branches, magnifying them mindlessly.
Dear heart, you've put a brave face on it, but know
exactly where the hugs and handshakes go.

Pantoum of the Emergency

for my father in Malaya, 1949–51

My genome has found itself put to the sword:
the broad steeled parang of the tropical wood.
It filmed itself chopping the heads off big wheels
because nobody carried a camera.

The broad steeled parang of the tropical wood
hacked outwards through vines and deep into my dreams.
Because nobody carried a camera
it handed me on the black baton of a grip.

Hacked outwards through vines and deep into my dreams,
the damage goes on as a jumpy loop tape.
It handed me on the black baton of a grip
like an article of night, like a roll of bad film.

The damage goes on, as a jumpy loop tape,
like a record run down in the tropical night,
like an article of night, like a roll of bad film
that the jungle has found its way into and spoilt.

Like a record run down in the tropical night,
the needle lifts off and the big night still plays.
That the jungle has found its way into and spoilt
a more temperate night is beyond any doubt.

The needle lifts off and the big night still plays.
The shock of still being there comes like an axe-fall.
A more temperate night is beyond any doubt.
Lightning is pink on the bedroom wall.

The shock of still being there comes like an axe-fall.
It screens itself chopping the heads off big wheels.
Lightning is pink. On the bedroom wall
my genome has found itself put to the sword.

Brutalist

Try living in one. Hang washing out to dry
and break its clean lines with your duds and smalls.
Spray tribal names across its subway walls
and crack its flagstones so the weeds can try

their damndest. That's the way. Fly-tip the lives
you led, out past its edge, on the back field;
sideboards and mangles made sense in the peeled-
spud light of the old house but the knives

are out for them now. This cellarless, unatticked
place will shake the rentman off, will throw
open its arms and welcome the White Arrow
delivery fleet which brings the things on tick

from the slush piles of the seasonal catalogues.
The quilt boxes will take up residence
on the tops of white wardrobes, an ambulance
raise blinds, a whole geography of dogs

will make their presence felt. And every year
on Le Corbusier's birthday, the sun will set
bang on the pre-ordained exact spot
and that is why we put that slab just there.

One by one the shopkeepers will shut
their doors for good. A newsagent will draw
the line at buttered steps. The final straw
will fill the fields beyond. Now live in it.

An Orrery of Hats

Everything in this display is moving
      and circling nearest to its sun are snoods
only meant to last a shift – they take
      hours to orbit. The party crowns
which see the light of day just once a year
      are meteoric, but if we stand well back
there's outer planets in the wings, top hats
      moving into a comet's night – we'll not
be seeing much more of them in our lifetimes
      though their sheen will come around again to grace
the evenings – and bonnets of beaverskin
      have reached the boreal brim; a naval rating's
peaked affair still has the salt-stained band
      from the night the ship went down with all hands,
sinking to the bottom of the clock;
      and look how many feathered confections float
as satellites that send no signal back,
      an entire species lost to a brief craze.
Passing through a belt of baseball caps, it's good
      to think of all the checks and tweeds sent up
as objects in a deep space probe, and hope
      that, on a night no one will live to see,
a deerstalker on its lonely course
      could provide the only clue to who we were
in some far corner of the universe.

Panda

SUSAN ASHE

She sat back on her haunches and seemed to be scratching herself. The scientists, who had her under surveillance, were worried about her, for, though she was in cub, she was very thin and disinclined to eat. Now, spurning a small clump of fresh bamboo, she sniffed the air. As if scenting something disagreeable, she lumbered off into the densest part of the undergrowth.

At midnight the moon rose, illuminating the bamboo forest, revealing that it was little more than a large grove in a dying landscape. But the night's brightness seemed to reanimate the panda. Hungrily she tore at a few leaves. She began to crunch them in her broad jaws, then, after a moment, unable to swallow her mouthful or sickened by it, she retched and spat out a green wad of half-digested matter.

Hours passed. In their homemade lair half a mile away, the scientists set up equipment to try to record the panda's nocturnal habits. A cry of pure savagery – the snarl of an ounce – came from the craggy mountains behind the forest. The men shivered. But the panda only lifted her head. In the pied light of the moon, her eyes were bruised with melancholy. One of the scientists reached for his notebook. Scribbling in it, he tried to express a notion which had come to him that her clown's colours made the panda's solitude more unbearable than ever. But he cancelled the sentence because the idea seemed fanciful.

Unseen, the panda headed out of the forest. When she reached the snowline she appeared to double in size and then to split, and it became evident that somewhere along the way she had been joined by a male. Together, the two animals made tracks through the snow, their flanks and their ringed eyes dark against the surrounding whiteness.

Around dawn, they came out onto a narrow ridge. Ahead of them, the mountains reared in a wild jumble of peaks and precipices. For some moments the two animals stood outlined against a greyish-mauve sky, then they vanished into the landscape.

Nearby, a team of photographers and their guides were searching for the pandas. The group had been living rough for three weeks and now they moved slowly and with difficulty. Each day they picked up the trail and followed it until nightfall. Each night, the pandas woke and marched until dawn. As yet, the team had not come in sight of the animals.

The guides were afraid. They knew that the female panda had eaten her latest cub and that the two adults were making for a cave high in the mountains, where they would die. Nothing could be done about this; it was the way of pandas. In the cave, angry at being followed to their secret place, they would turn back into demons. Then they would disguise themselves as pandas and come down the mountain and terrorise the village. Everyone knew, including the demons, that it was against the law to kill pandas. The animals would maraud without fear.

'The pandas are starving,' the woman photographer said to the guides. ' They are going to die. That is why they are making for the cave.'

'Yes,' the chief guide said. 'They will die but they will be reborn. It is the destiny of pandas.'

'Pandas do not molest man or woman or cattle or sheep,' the woman said. 'They eat only bamboo. The bamboo is dying. The bamboo always dies. It may be that it is too late to save any pandas, but with our photographs we must try.'

The guide saw that these photographers could not tell the difference between pandas and demons. He fell silent.

'Take us to the cave,' the head photographer said. 'Then the two of you can go down and join the rest of the party at the snowline. If we are not back in four days, you must come up and look for us.'

One of the guides pointed to a dark smudge on a rock face. That, he said, was the pandas' cave. He knew because, caught out in a storm, he had once sheltered there. The cave was full of panda bones. The photographers thanked the guides. They left, dropping out of sight behind the steep angle of the mountain.

The next day, the photographers climbed towards where the guide had pointed and set up a tent. Then they entered the cave. It was dark as a tomb. The team leader, a tall thin man, shone a torch, muffling its beam with his fingers.

'Look at that,' gasped the other man, a shortish fellow with a beard.

The other two followed his pointed finger. In the depths of the cave a magnificent heap of white and black-brown fur lay motionless. Two pairs of eyes gleamed in the darkness.

'God, aren't they beautiful,' the woman breathed. 'I can't bear to think of them lying there until they die.'

'Couldn't we feed them?' the bearded man asked.

The tall man shook his head. 'They wouldn't eat. And even if they don't die now they'll soon starve anyway.'

The three fell silent. After a while, the bearded man said, 'How long do they have?' He seemed agitated, stroking his beard continually as if the act might calm him down.

'About a week,' the woman said. 'Then wolves will get them.'

'So it could be any day?'

The woman nodded. 'They're very weak or they would never have let us get so near.'

The bearded man controlled himself with an effort. Slowly, he advanced into the cave. The pandas watched him. He crept forward a yard at a time. Stretching out a hand, he touched the flank of the male animal.

The female twitched an ear.

'She's still alive,' the woman whispered. 'Come on, let's get started.'

At the mouth of the cave, the tall man and the woman busied themselves with their cameras. From time to time, the bearded man, who had remained beside the pandas, put his gloved hand to his face as if he could not bear to look at the dying animals.

All morning the woman and the thin man moved about the cave, shooting from every angle. In the afternoon, while it was still light, they went outside and took shots of the scenery. Then a wind blew up, and the weather began to close in. They called to their companion, and the three made their way down to their tent under a sky purple with snow.

In the tent, the tall man heated water over a stove and dropped bouillon cubes into three tin mugs. When the water boiled, he filled the mugs and handed them round.

'We shall have to sit it out,' he said, rummaging in a bag, and pulled out some sausages. 'We've got enough food for about five days. The storm can't last that long.'

The other two sipped their soup.

'I can't bear it,' the woman said after a while. 'I just can't. Those superb animals.'

'What I don't understand is why they came up here,' the tall man said. 'The guide said there was enough food in the forest for one pair but that these two, the only ones left, seemed to have given up.'

'If an animal were starving, wouldn't it eat whatever it could get hold of?' the bearded man asked.

'I don't think so,' the tall man said. 'It wouldn't know it was food.'

Again the three fell silent, gloomily stirring their mugs.

'This reminds me so much of that time in the Kalahari when we came across the old bushman couple,' the woman said to the tall man.

His face clouded over and he looked uncomfortable. 'They knew what was going to happen to them,' he said. 'It was their custom. This is not at all the same thing.'

'What was going to happen?' the bearded man said.

'They were too old and frail to keep up with the tribe,' the woman told him. 'So the others built them a shelter and gave them an ostrich eggshell full of water.' She ran her hands through her hair. 'The old people just lay there. They knew lions would soon get them.'

The wind had been rising steadily, and the woman had to shout.

The bearded man raised his voice. 'What did you do?'

'We offered them food, but they didn't seem to notice it. It was as if, because the tribal custom said they had to die, death was the only thing they could see. We put them in the truck and headed for the nearest town.'

'What happened to the old couple?'

'They died on the way.'

'So you never got your picture.'

The tall man jerked up his head. 'What picture?'

'The one of them being torn apart by lions?'

This time the silence was jagged.

The thin man began to cook. He stirred sausages on the stove. 'You're in this too,' he said. 'These pandas are going to die, and we're just here to record the event.'

The bearded man was not listening. He had begun to pull string after string of sausages out of the bag. Struggling into his snowsuit, he stuffed the sausages down inside the jacket. Then he fastened his hood and plunged out into the snowstorm.

'For God's sake!' The thin man threw himself after his friend.

'Don't be a fool,' the woman said, pulling the thin man back inside. As she spoke, a gust struck the tent, almost tearing it apart. The man and the woman gazed at each other. The wind racked itself up another notch, and a desolate shriek came whistling down the mountains.

The storm blew for six days. When it subsided, the sun came out. It fingered its way into the cave, where the she-panda opened her eyes. Her ears twitched faintly and then she took a deep breath. With a supreme effort, she heaved herself to her feet and crept towards the mouth of the cave.

Outside, the snow was dazzling. All the contours had vanished. The female panda took a few steps, her nose low. Stopping, she began with her last gram of strength to dig. Deeper she went, and deeper. A man's face gleamed palely up at her. The panda sniffed, lowered her muzzle to the man's chest and began to tear at his red suit.

The heat of the dying man's body had kept the sausages from freezing solid, and now the panda's hot breath warmed them. She tore into them. Finding nothing else on the stiff scarlet body, she made her way towards the buried tent, following her now faultless nose. Here, she ate her fill of sausages, tearing them out of the fastened kitbag. Then, catching the last string in her teeth, she set off back towards the cave.

The male had little more than the strength to open an eye when the she-panda dropped the sausages in front of him. For a while he sniffed at them, just as he had at the dying bamboo. Then he too began to eat.

Some hours later, the sun now plunging behind the derelict forest, the pandas lumbered back down below the snowline. They continued their route for several days, stopping only to eat a few sheep and goats that had been penned up in a mountain hovel. The herdsman ran off, gibbering with fear.

The pandas made their way down the mountain until, above a village, near a stream, they found a dry niche among the rocks. Here they rested. That night, they went down to the village and ate two cows, a cowherd and a dog. Then they disappeared back up to their den.

By the end of two months, the pandas were fit and healthy. As well as another small flock of sheep, they had eaten a woman and her old father, who had gone out together to find what was preying on their animals. The female panda was in cub.

Some time passed before news leaked out, because the villagers – knowing they were dealing with demons – were not surprised at what had happened. Afraid of angering the demons still further, they refused to answer questions but attempted to appease the demons by staking goats out on the hillside.

It was decided by the authorities and people from the outside that bandits had done the killings. Or jealous neighbours. A couple of villagers were marched off. The she-panda was sighted again. The scientists saw her eating bamboo shoots. She slept much of the time, they reported. But this was the way of pandas.

Three Versions from Rilke's
Sonnets to Orpheus

DON PATERSON

Tone

Only one who's also raised
his lyre among the shades
may live to render up the praise
that will not fail or fade.

Only one who tasted death's
own flower on his lips
can keep that tone as light as breath
beneath his fingertips.

Though its reflection starts to swim
before your failing sight:
know the image.

Only in the double realm
is the voice both infinite
and assuaged.

The Yellow Nib, Vol. 2, 2006, pp. 12–14
© Don Paterson

Time

Is there really such thing as time-the-destroyer?
When will it shatter the tower on the rock?
When will that low demiurge overpower
this heart, that runs only to heaven's clock?

Are we really so fragile, so easily broken
as fate wants to prove us, or have us believe?
Is the infinite life that our childhood awakened
torn up by the roots, and then thrown in the grave?

Look how the ghosts of impermanence slide
straight through the mind of the open receiver
again and again, like smoke through a tree.

Among the Eternal – wherein we reside
as that which we truly are, the urgent, the strivers –
we still count; as their means, as their Earth-agency.

The Cry

The call of one lone bird can make us cry –
whatever sounds just once, then dies away.
But listen: beyond the mere sound of their play,
those kids playing beneath the open sky –

they cry the *chance!* They hammer every scream
like a wedge into the black interstices
of the world . . . Those cracks where only the bird-cries
pass clean through, the way men do in dreams.

O, where are we now? Freer and freer,
like kites torn from their lines, we loop and race
in the middle air . . . Our tattered hems snicker

like lunatics . . . O lord, make one great choir
of all the criers, so they wake as one voice,
one current, carrying both the head and lyre!

For a Few Dollars More

FRANCIS O'HARE

'Don't talk much. Don't much see the need.
Figure as long as there's gonna be shootin'
Won't be a whole lotta time for hat-doffin'.
Never met a man yet whose blood
Came out of him all hollerin' and hootin'.
Maybe you'd best get ready some coffins.'
That's what he said, sure as I'm standin' here
And I felt somethin' then, somethin' like fear.

He was over six foot, wore a Mexican poncho,
Smoked a cheroot, not young, but old neither.
Seemed to be somehow lookin' over his shoulder.
Went by no name, no, wait now, Manquo . . .
or Joe . . . or Blondie . . . as dry as the weather
When it came to my questions, blue eyes colder
Than Missouri in winter . . . hell, like I said,
A man you'd've thought was back from the dead.

Booked into the hotel across the street there,
It's run by some midget came out from the East
The time of the gold-strike . . . hell, that didn't last . . .
Stayed two days in his room, didn't go nowhere.
Then, the third day, the day of the feast
To welcome back Indio, his long shadow cast
A pall on the veranda . . . that was the start
Of the trouble that tore this damned town apart.

The Yellow Nib, Vol. 2, 2006, pp. 15–24
© Francis O'Hare

There'd been rumours, of course, of San Miguel;
How the Rojos and Baxters ended up underground
By acceptin' the hand of a mysterious friend
Who spread death faster than typhoid or cholera,
How the place became a burial mound
And how he went ridin' off, right at the end,
Smilin' peacefully, like savin' their souls
Was how he saw fillin' people with holes.

But this place was long past heedin' black omens.
A circle of buzzards or a coyote's howl
Were as familiar round here as a funeral bell.
What, with all of the gunfire; widows, orphans
And the gaunt ghost-face of the Franciscan cowl
Made the poor streets seem like a picture of hell.
No, if ever a Sodom needed a dark saviour,
This was the spot. And him our deliverer.

And now Indio was back from bein' on the run
From the Mexican army for rapin' the daughter
Of some high-up government official or other
Whom he'd taken a shine to while robbin' a train.
He'd hidden out for a year over the border
In a saloon run by, it's rumoured, his mother,
Though the truth of the thing, as far as I know,
Is the joint was more of a low-life bordello.

And Indio the son of a juiced Texan cowpoke
And a bitch señorita, which explains a whole lot;
How one of his eyes was blacker than soot
While the other was blue as a Winchester's smoke,
And that's just the start; why he just seemed to hate
Anything livin' he couldn't own or shoot.
Which is why that day the town held its breath
And waited for drinkin', gunplay and death.

The sun hung in the sky like a lynchin',
Flies buzzin' round noon like it's started to rot.
His shadow dug out a grave in the street
As he crossed over to Indio's mansion.
I'm referrin', of course, to the stranger, not
That I doubt you're aware of that, but
To follow this story as straight as an arrow
Our path will sometimes get crooked and narrow.

Indio's men were all out in the front yard
Drinkin' tequila and pickin' out women
From the wives of the locals. Someone was strummin'
Flamenco tunes on a guitar which soared
Into the air, like an old Latin mass hymn.
Then, in chorus, a bullet would go hummin'
Into the wide blue, like a message to God.
'Keep out of this, hombre,' it most likely said.

Then, everythin' stopped, like a clockwork scene
You see advertised in the papers sometimes.
You know the type, all tinkles and chimes,
Paul Revere's Ride, or *Saint George and the Dragon*,
'Miracles of invention', the small print claims.
Or, at least, until the lost windin' key dooms
Them all to an eternity locked in themselves.
And that's what happens when fate calmly arrives

In the figure walking straight out of the fire
Of the midday sun. I mention the gew-gaw
By way of alludin' to Indio's familiar,
A musical timepiece cast in fine silver
He used to torture his victims with, makin' them draw
When the delicate tune was finally over,
Only to blow them away to Kingdom Come
With a flick of the wrist and a smile of aplomb.

But this day was different. Before they awoke
From whatever sleep it was they'd fallen prey to,
He'd sent three to Hell. The others could see
Similar ends and weren't keen to provoke
His trigger just yet. They waited for Indio
To appear in the doorway. Ages went by
Before their leader, in full bandito regalia,
Emerged from the shadows, drinkin' tequila

And lookin' like murder was most on his mind.
'Howdee,' our friend says, lightin' a cheroot,
'I thought it was time I paid my respects.'
Well, that's it, I thought, this is the end,
But no, I was wrong. 'I've brought you the loot
From the bank in El Paso. The others were picked
Off in an ambush. I'd say there's a posse,
Twenty or so riders, headed this way.'

And with that, like a twister that just misses town,
The mood changed to laughter, drinkin' and talkin'.
I just stood there, dumbstupefied, blinkin'
And rubbin' my eyes, as if to wipe clean a pane
Of glass I'd been lookin' through darkly. Somethin'
Was wrong with this. Somethin' was wrong in
The way Indio smiled and clapped arms around
A stranger who smiled back like his oldest friend.

'We'll head north, through the desert, let's go!'
Indio's horse was saddled and ready,
As it always was, for any unseen emergency,
And he led the whole band, includin' one Manquo,
In a duststorm of hooves into the red eye
Of the afternoon sun. The town was left empty
To welcome the long arm of the law
With the dead-eyed look of a Comanche squaw . . .

A month or so later they arrived back in town,
Hungry and thirsty as a pack of grey wolves,
With faces that told of cold nights in the caves
Of the mountains, where the temperature goes down
To well below freezin', and days that no salves
Or ointments would cure, under the fierce gaze
Of the skies of the badlands. These men were cursed
By seein' their future and fearin' the worst.

And what was their guilt? Well, the one figure missin'
Was most likely the best man to figure that mystery.
The stranger was gone! His name was a memory
They laughed over that night, recallin' the questions
Indio had asked him about his past history
Before, blood-streaked, they tied him up like a delivery
To his own horse and sent him into the desert
To make peace with his maker, or die in the effort.

See, Indio had known from the start that our friend
Wasn't all he appeared. With his uncanny slant eye
For pickin' out lawmen or hunters of bounty
He'd weighed up the odds and all along planned
For the time in the wilderness, knowin' that Blondie
Would make a move soon, and that back in the town he
Had too many options in his cool game of chess
That relied on shadows and mistaken vendettas.

Not in the open, though, under the heavens.
There, he was no one, just another poor sinner
To be sent to oblivion by a 45's hammer,
To suffer the injustice of the blue skies, driven
On the roads to nowhere, riddled with hunger
And the merciless light of a swelterin' summer.
This was his punishment, Indio declared,
For goin' straight to Hell in search of reward.

And here you'd expect I've finished my tale.
But more was to follow before the next dawn.
Clouds unwrapped themselves from the moon
Like weeds off a corpse that has risen from all
The darkness of the crypt, and given a yawn,
Before walkin' out past the burial stone
Into the world of the livin', as the bandits
Retired to their lairs, all swappin' dark glances.

And then, when the night had entered the shadow
Of the valley of death, a pistol-shot sang
A lament that woke every man from his dreamin'
Of a land of milk and honey. Tomorrow
The street would resemble, as the church bells rang,
One of the towns in the Civil War, bleedin',
It seemed, from a thousand fresh wounds.
The pale rider was back! Indio was doomed!

Mornin' arrived under a blood-red sky.
The sun was a bullet hole. Dozens lay dead,
Piled in the street like tipped-up loads
Of dung, or dirt. The mansion was empty.
The windows were broken. The horses had fled
Into the night at the first sound of explod-
in' dynamite. An unearthly silence
Was the only survivor of the night before's violence.

But I can tell you the truth of what happened.
Or as close to the truth as you need to know.
I might play with the facts some, like the newspaper motto:
When the legend becomes fact, print the legend.
But it's beauty I'm after, like the poet, Longfellow,
When he wrote that moonshine, what's it called, *Hiawatha?*
And maybe I'm not a professor at Harvard,
But in my line you get close to the wanderin' spirits.

And that's what he was, a spirit or ghost,
The way he came out of the dark to play tricks
On Indio's crew. The first fell for a hoax –
Light laughin' somewhere out in the mist.
The second died clutchin' a gold crucifix
He'd ripped from the throat of God-fearin' folks.
The third, beckoned at knife-point to join the Hereafter,
Bled quickly away, like Manquo's dry laughter.

And the rest were to follow. Next, an explosion
Scattered the horses and lit up the night
Like Fourth of July fireworks, over a woodcut
Scene from Saint John's Book of Revelations;
Fire and brimstone, smoke, burnt cordite,
And God separatin' the sheep and the goats
As his shadow, the Beast, the hungry fiend's lips
Screamed from every corner this was Apocalypse.

And through this nightmare the stranger went,
Steppin' over the dead, through the dead air,
His poncho slung, pitchfork-like, over his shoulder,
Less for use, you might say, than pure devilment.
But his madness had method. He haunted their leader
Like the whale haunted Ahab, a ghost-pale spectre
In the ocean of darkness and doom that he sailed on,
Holed up in the hacienda, awaitin' the showdown.

The mansion was like somethin' out of Irving or Poe.
Bad things had gone on in that house in the past.
Men had gone in there before heading west
Like Ichabod Crane, you've read *Sleepy Hollow*?
Headless, I mean, only this time the ghost-
Horseman was Indio's unwelcome guest.
Yes, Indio's place that night was as black
As the heart of the palace in the midst of the plague

Where Prospero held the Masque of the Red Death.
As the story goes, the most westward chamber
Was draped in black velvet and lit by a brazier
That shone through blood-tinted panes, like the breath
Of pestilence stalking every last corner
Of Prospero's dukedom, bringin' death and despair
To all in its path. I mention these stories
To give you a sense of the place and its history.

I seem to recall there was also a clock,
Fashioned from ebony, that tolled for the prince.
Well, remember I mentioned Indio's timepiece,
The one wrought from silver he kept for good luck?
Well, it ticked too, through the deafenin' silence
In the wake of our pilgrim's bloodthirsty progress,
As Indio dreamt ways of sidesteppin' his doom
In some moonlit and florid inner sanctum.

And, all the while, Blondie sat smokin'
An endless supply of dirty cheroots
And spittin' tobacco through the slit of his teeth.
He was waitin', I guess, for the onset of dawn,
Strikin' his matches off one of his boots
And watchin' for anythin' that moved on the street.
But, as yet, there was nothin' to see but the vultures
That appeared along rooftops, it seemed, out of nowhere.

And that brings us back to the spot where I wandered
Off the path of uprightness. Never mind.
What does the poet say? *On a huge hill Truth stands*
And he that will reach her . . . Well, that mornin', the wonder
Sun-up revealed in the street was the kind
To shock the spirits of all but the damned.
I suppose, though, that Indio now felt like the angel
Who fell out of Paradise and landed in Hell.

That's the only way to explain his bravado.
Either that or the bottle of whiskey he held,
As he half-staggered out, into the cold
Light of day, casting an uncertain shadow.
But somethin' possessed him as he straightened and smiled.
'Amigo, it worked. Our plan worked,' he called
Across the gulf between himself and the calm
And collected man with no name.

Was this another twist in the plot?
I told you this tale was worse than a rattlesnake's.
Had the two of them formed an unholy alliance
To carve up the others and then carve the loot?
By this time I was tired of makin' mistakes
In 'cipherin' what went on in the brains
Of these bitter, violent men. Like climbin' the stair
That winds up to the noose and the drop through thin air.

But Indio had taken one gamble too many.
'Open the timepiece,' was all he got back
By way of an answer. I could hear the blood tick
In the back of my head like a runaway symphony,
As the two of them waited for the timepiece to lock
And bring to an end that still, sad music,
But all I could do was watch how their eyes
Seemed to catch fire from the hot desert skies.

And then it was over. In a huge thunderclap
Indio lay shattered, dead, facedown
In the dirt of the street, as the traveller moved on,
Not sayin' a word, just saddlin' up
And driftin' off over the lone, level plain
Into the consumin' flame of the sun.
He rode straight out of history, into this legend,
A wanderin' outlaw of his own dark mind.

And that's how it happened, as true as I stand,
An old man waitin', in a dry new century,
For death to take him. It's years now since Blondie
Blew through our town like a wind off the wasteland.
In the peace that followed, we welcomed prosperity;
Saloons, banks, brothels, the railroad company –
They swarmed in like flies after a Civil War battle
To lay eggs in the guts of the dead. Unreal.

King Kong

ALAN GILLIS

When W.B. Yeats sounded out the climax of 'Byzantium' in 1930 – 'That dolphin-torn, that gong-tormented sea' – he was clearly on the same wavelength as the creators of the looming Eighth Wonder of the World. Unlike the mutual rise and fall of 'ding-dong', or the easy swing and fold of 'sing-song', 'King Kong' tintinnabulates discordantly. 'Kong' takes 'King' and turns it inside out, warping it through the hollow of its 'o'. 'Kong' reverbs with the implicit violence of 'King', the ring of its 'ng' become a wrong, its majesty gorilla-torn, kong-tormented.

Yeats wrote that a symbol should have 'numberless meanings besides the one or two the writer lays an emphasis upon, or the half-score he knows of', and the makers of *King Kong* complied. The 1933 film is habitually credited to Edgar Wallace and Merian C. Cooper. Edgar Wallace had signed a scriptwriting deal with RKO in December 1931, the first project assigned to him being Cooper's *The Beast*. However, he died in February 1932 without contributing 'one bloody word', according to Cooper. Thus Wallace's name remained linked with the project purely for the kudos he provided, having penned *The Angel of Terror*, *The Feathered Serpent* and *The Dark Eyes of London*.

Merian C. Cooper had hunted Pancho Villa with the National Guard. As a pilot he was shot down over Poland during World War One. Then, having recuperated, he was shot down again, spending nine months in a Soviet POW camp. He would later be a member of the Flying Tigers in China. And, in partnership with Ernst Schoedsack, he was the intrepid maker of exotic 'nature dramas'. At a time when David Attenborough and Steven Spielberg might as

The Yellow Nib, Vol. 2, 2006, pp. 25–34
© Alan Gillis

well have been one and the same person, Cooper captured vivid beasts and unclad natives with his lens, specialising in splicing real footage with staged events. The finale of *Chang* (1927) erupted with an elephant stampede.

Meanwhile, in 1926, William Douglas Burden, a trustee of the American Museum of Natural History, travelled to Indonesia to film and capture a Komodo dragon. He described his first encounter: '[He] approached step by step, the great bulk of his body held clear off the ground . . . the black beady eyes flashing in their deep sockets . . . black as dead lava.' 'Occasionally,' wrote Burden, the dragon 'stopped and raised himself on those iron forelegs to look around.' 'Nearer he came and nearer . . . with grim head swinging heavily from side to side. I remembered all the fantastic stories I had heard of these creatures attacking both men and horses, and was in no way reassured. Now listening to the short hissing that came like a gust of evil wind, and observing the action of that darting, snake-like tongue . . . I was affected in a manner not easy to relate.'

Given the success of a 1925 film version of Arthur Conan Doyle's *The Lost World*, the fact that such monsters were real and available for photography was cinematic gold dust, making potential audiences wonder what other rare beasts might be out there, slouching through undiscovered tropics. What is more, when Burden brought back two live dragons and housed them in Bronx Zoo, they died. Correspondence indicated that Burden attributed their death to modern civilisation. At the same time Cooper, aware of Burden's dragons, began dreaming of a giant gorilla wreaking havoc through Manhattan, and *The Beast* was born.

The next most significant creator of Kong was George O'Brien, the Godfather of stop-motion animation. O'Brien was known as OBie and was thus responsible for Obi-Wan Kenobi (George Lucas was a fan). A tragic figure – during the shooting of *Son of Kong* in late 1933 his ill wife shot and killed their two sons and then turned the gun on herself, only to drain her tubercular lung and desperately extend her asylum-bound life – O'Brien had been responsible for the magic behind *The Lost World*, and was feverishly working on dinosaurs for a Darwinian epic called *Creation*. Cooper, head full with gorillas, was called in and immediately saw an opening, claiming *Creation* was unfeasible but that its sets, and O'Brien's labours, could still be used. And so the ex-pugilist puppet-master would spend the next year choreographing Kong's punch-ups, leading one Kongologist to rhapsodise: '[Y]ou find yourself imagining the additional dimension that exists "between seconds" onscreen; OBie repositioning the great ape ever so slightly and disappearing from frame, thousands of times, again and again, hour after hour, resulting in a minute and a half of movie life.' In this way, an eighteen-inch metal frame padded with rubber and covered with rabbit fur became an abomination that had audiences fainting in the aisles.

The visual heart of the film lies in the way the beast's dreamlike movements are set against painterly fantasias, as the hallucinogenically menacing motions of Kong's dark form are relieved by hazily swayed jungle and emulsive skies. In 1933 it was feared *King Kong* might induce heart attacks, aisle stampedes and mass hysteria. Now the film's impact has shifted to less abrupt but deeper channels of myth-kitsch. Now *King Kong* excites not just nostalgia for defunct technology – although no other effects-driven film of the era comes close to wielding the same time-melting, otherworldly power – but an instinctual submission to the idiosyncratic and iconic aura of the puppet himself. Because Kong fails to resemble a real gorilla, because he is a mound of bristled rabbit fur with comedy eyes and cartoon anthropomorphics, and because he stalks his domain with such trancelike motions, he truly is Lord of a dream realm, a lost dimension that overlaps but transmogrifies our own.

It is difficult to surmise how interested and aware of *King Kong*'s 'meaning' Cooper might have been. The motto of Cooper-Schoedsack Productions was 'Keep it Distant, Difficult and Dangerous', and it seems Cooper was driven to produce a wham-bam roller coaster that would stun with its techno-visual oomph and rake in a fortune. But he was surely not blind to Kong's symbolic prowess. Moreover, Cooper's two scriptwriters, James Creelman and Ruth Rose (Delos W. Lovelace handled the story's 'novelisation'), may well have extended the tale's allegorical boundaries while satisfying Cooper's need for cinematic speed.

In any case, it seems clear that *King Kong* was imaged with set themes in mind. Fay Wray's character, Ann Darrow, Kong's true love and the cause of his fall, is named after Clarence Darrow, attorney in the so-called Monkey Trial of 1925, concerning a teacher's right to teach evolution to children (an anti-evolution law prohibited scientists from testifying in favour of evolution). In terms of race, the fact that Kong goes for the blonde, after years of native maidens, says it all. Fay Wray's onscreen hysteria plays out contemporary nightmares of miscegenation, while Kong's subversive eroticism reaches its peak when, unleashed in New York, he peeping-Toms through a bedroom window to disturb a bourgeois woman's breath-heavy dreams.

Kong stands for unrestrained power, fury and instinct; primal masculinity; an id that partakes of the Christian man's outrage at seeing a monkey in the mirror; the white man's horror at seeing a black man in the mirror; his terror of white women in arms of darkness. But we are also, of course, in the heart of the Great Depression, and Kong is the rage of the poor and dispossessed, the failure of the system striking back, the repressed returned to raze the capital. And so the film begins to spin our points of identification on their head. Kong is a noble and brave protector, steadfast and true. Kong contains his contradictions. Peter Conrad writes: 'King Kong connects our origins in the swamp with our ambition to reconquer heaven by building towers of Babel; it is about atavism and aspiration, and, when the monster starts to fancy his screaming female captive, it forces us to rethink the divisions we have made between animal, man and god.'

King Kong is a film that feverously exploits our lust for sensation and exploitation, while evangelistically condemning such lust. King Kong is a film about making a film of King Kong. It puts a huge beast on screen at which we confabulate, shriek and ogle; then it shows the beast chained to a stage at which an audience confabulates, shrieks and ogles; and then it savages that audience, the stage-directors, and the entire practice of ogling. King Kong puts a super-beast of extraordinary power atop the highest building on earth, then shoots him down. It's a parable about the cost and cruelty of technological progress, which turns the cinema into a dealer of weirdly detached hi-tech hits.

Watching the original King Kong on TV in Pukerua Bay in 1973, Peter Jackson's 12-year-old eyes popped out of his head, and he instantly dedicated his life to making films, beginning with a remake of Kong, using cereal packets and kitchen utensils, which he filmed in a back shed. He went on to make his name with *Bad Taste* (1987), in which aliens invade a New Zealand village in order to harvest human beings for their intergalactic fast-food franchise but are repelled by a four-man paramilitary force. Jackson himself played two roles – a key scene shows one character played by Jackson torture the other. Also, one website informs us: 'This film may have established the exploding sheep concept in the computer gaming subculture.' Jackson followed this with *Meet the Feebles* (1989), a puppet film modelled on Jim Henson's *Muppets* and featuring prurient drug-taking scenes, puppet porn, date rape, and a snuff film within the film. Soon after, he made *Brain Dead* (1992), a zombie comedy considered by many the goriest film ever made, focusing on the dangers of the Sumatran Rat-Monkey, found on Skull Island. After that, a few financial successes finally earned him a budget kongtastic enough to make his career turn full circle.

The most striking thing about Jackson's *King Kong* (2005), the most expensive film ever made, is its size. The film showcases a new peak in computer-generated imagery and lavishes itself upon a gargantuan canvas. Charles Brooker writes: 'If there'd been a scene in which Kong went to the toilet, it would've run like this: 1) Kong unfurls his 10km penis and piddles into an erupting volcano for 45 minutes; 2) Kong turns around and passes a stool the size of a blue whale, in slow motion, to the strains of a 20,000-strong choir, while Naomi Watts stares at him, her eyes brimming with love; 3) his bowels emptied, Kong plucks the planet Jupiter out of the sky and swallows it for no reason, while fighting 15 giant crocodiles. And a robot. And a pig.'

Some details from the film's production notes are worth recounting. Jackson wanted 'an exaggerated design, whose realism has been supplanted by painterly extreme'. To create the film's jungle, his team created 104,000 pieces of artificial foliage; 3,100 latex vines; 1,500 fabric vines; 25,000 live miniature-scale plants; 120 miniature-scale articulated trees; 100 miniature-scale non-articulated trees; and a plethora of root systems, bark texture panels, mosses and other flora. Rather than go contemporary, the film is set

back in 1933, so, to create the film's city, Jackson's team 'rebuilt'
57,468 unique Manhattan buildings, with another 32,839 for
Queens, Brooklyn and New Jersey, covering an area stretching more
than 26 miles. All of these were 3-D constructions with newly
created software allowing one to take a camera and fly anywhere in
the virtual city.

Jackson was adamant that his Kong would not be a monster but a
silverback gorilla who happens to be 25 feet tall and weigh 8,000
pounds. Andy Serkis, the actor behind Gollum – the cinema's most
advanced digital film character, pre-Kong 2005 – was duly cast.
Trusting that his character would have 'an emotional arc', Serkis
researched Charles Laughton's Quasimodo, spent a lot of time in
London Zoo, and travelled to observe the mountain gorillas in
Rwanda. When taken to Jackson's studio, Serkis had his face pinned
with motion-capture markers connected to software which translated
his facial expressions into corresponding gorilla expressions. Serkis
also acted out the role of Kong for his fellow thespians, 'providing on-
set reference and functioning as an emotionally present participant in
the scenes', in a custom-made Kong-suit. To make this more real,
Jackson's sound department developed a 'Kongalizer' that took Serkis's
vocal responses, ran them through a computer, and then broadcast
them through a wall of speakers in real time. In the end, Jackson's
team studied Serkis's performance, and then studied gorilla behaviour
independently, blending the two to create the ultimate Kong.

The result is startling. Marianne Moore once suggested poetry
should provide 'imaginary gardens with real toads in them'. Jackson's
film gives us a Nintendo game with a real, 25-foot, mad gorilla in it,
making De Niro's Jake La Motta look like Bambi. This Kong is a
wildly physical, heartpoundingly brutal vision, a gibbous ball of feral
muscle; surely the most extraordinary technological feat the cinema
has yet produced.

However, the film does not rush. Indeed, the first hour drags its
way into deep dramatic stodge, which is a startling contrast with
what follows, because once the Venture hits Skull Island, the screen
rockets. The natives of the island greet the crew by staving their
heads in on merciless rocks in the bleak chill of a lurid rainstorm
(until they spot the blonde). This creates a bloodcurdling tone that

drives the ensuing super-real momentum, as Jackson's computerised phantasmagoria tumefies into a scopophilic orgy. Jackson even had his 'real' actors scanned to create digital doubles (the cross-simulation of skin texture was painstaking) so he could throw them off cliffs with abandon and have them stomped by stampeding brontosaurs, or eaten by swarming moonspiders and megapedes. The eye cannot keep up as Kong pinball-machines a Vastatosaurus Rex, then another, then another, and then takes on three at once, while doubling as a trapeze artist who juggles his maiden like a colossal, furry Errol Flynn.

Given its scale, it's hardy surprising that Jackson's Kongathon draws out more nuanced elements of the King's mythology. In this, of course, Jackson was helped by 70-odd years of Kongology. Reflecting changing times and values, Dino de Laurentis's *King Kong* (1976) had already cast Carl Denham – the Merian C. Cooper character of the film – as the unambiguous villain of the piece (an oil prospector), while Kong was seen as 'a Christ-like symbol of the pure, moral being done in by greedy, unprincipled men'. Dino's film had Kong climb the Twin Towers rather than the Empire State Building, leading *Time* magazine to opine in the issue of 25 October 1976: 'That final destructive binge could be seen – and lines in the script lightly suggest it – as a projection of Western fears of what might happen if the Third World should develop its potential power and strike back.'

An earlier film had taken the twin ideas of Kong-as-nature and Kong-as-protector to their logical limit. In *Kingukongu no gyakushu* (1967) an evil scientist, Dr Hu, plans to take over the world by building a huge 'Mechni Kong', a robot modelled on Kong, designed to put the real thing out of commission while flattening civilisation. Needless to say, only Kong can save the day. Meanwhile, a sequel to the 1976 film, *King Kong Lives* (1986), gives us the premise that Kong survived his fall from the Twin Towers, and has spent the last ten years lying in a coma in a university research centre outside Atlanta. A big game hunter discovers a female Kong in the jungles of Borneo and transports her to the research centre for a transfusion that will enable Kong to have an artificial heart transplant. But romance blooms between the two Kongs, and they make a bid for freedom.

In such a vein, Jackson invests heavily in Kong's emotional arc.

Naomi Watts's Ann Darrow is a vaudeville dancer and, in a moment of desperation, she takes to tap-dancing and cartwheeling to entertain Kong. Skull Island thus becomes the Court and Banquet Hall in which a subject is made to clown for her tyrant and master – a scene made visually stunning through the contrast of their sizes and hirsuteness. More importantly, Kong goes ape when Darrow finishes through tiredness, hysterically demanding that she dance on and on. This impresses upon us his loutish aggression and instinctive despotism, but also swerves the film onto new emotional terrain, for this tantrum reveals Kong's innermost character: he's a big baby – the most awful, destructive toddler ever committed to celluloid.

As the *Venture* drifts off the map towards Skull Island, Jackson has one shipmate read *Heart of Darkness*. But if Kong is the real Kurtz, this film implies, then the secret, true, rancid nature of civilisation stems from our repression of our inner two-year-old. And if this is, in theory, merely Freud-by-numbers, Kong provides a uniquely visceral magnification of the nappy-wearing, waddling, guzzling, emotionally destabilised, possessive, rampant monstrosity that we all barely contain within ourselves, erupting onscreen with complex ferocity.

Jackson described his Kong in these terms: 'He's a very lonely creature – absolutely solitary. It must be one of the loneliest existences you could ever possibly imagine. Every day, he has to battle for his survival against very formidable dinosaurs on the island, and it's not easy for him. He's carrying the scars of many former encounters with dinosaurs . . . And he has never felt a single bit of empathy for another living creature in his long life.' And so, at the heart of the film, as our hero remorselessly pounds through whatever stands in his way to possess Darrow, wreaking wholesale murder and mayhem wherever he goes, it becomes clear that Kong wants his mammy.

This undercuts any sense that Naomi Watts's Ann Darrow is a pervert, as she gazes deep into Kong's black, fervid eyes. Rather, her desires are maternal and just – just a little misplaced. Moreover, this endows Kong's climactic killing on the phallic precipice with a great emotional wallop, as the might of America's military–industrial machine is coldly and inexorably turned against our oversized, overexcited, overwhelmed, but innocent infant. Essentially, the film's conclusion presents us with a virtual two-year-old being repeatedly shot by machine-gun fire because of a temper wobble. Emotionally, we are traumatised; intellectually, we see the necessity.

Such necessity eludes those eco-Kong critics who sentimentalise the King's fate into a one-dimensional parable of the destruction of nature. This reading evades the undesirability of having a vast gorilla indulge in a human-killing frenzy. Even back on Skull Island, although Jackson gives us scenes of Kong chowing down on his sustainable tree-shoot dinner, gazing serenely at a widescreen paradise-advertisement image of the sun setting on high-definition horizons, Kong mostly rules through terror. Apart from Darrow, there is not one living creature that crosses his path whose skull he doesn't crunch, or whose neck he doesn't wring within his hairy hammer-like arms.

Not to kill Kong would be grossly negligent. If Kong is nature, nature is a serial killer, a riot of death. A repulsion–attraction dynamic is thus the engine motoring *King Kong*. Kong is a deeply dialectical behemoth. In the contemporary context, Kong is a jihad against the West, a dark Other wielding inexplicable violence. As such, from Hollywood's perspective, the film's triumphant aeroplanes are the righteous West striking back. But Kong also doubles as George W. Bush. Kong symbolises a tyrannical will-to-power blindly hitting out at a world it cannot understand.

Kong's ultimate meaning is bound up with the wonder and horror of technology. While the aeroplanes and tower symbolise humanity's technological accomplishment, Kong atop the tower swatting the planes symbolises a primal emotional failure to submit to such complexity, or to the diminishment of individual powers which that complexity entails.

Kong is terror, and *King Kong* is terror as primetime entertainment. The medium is the message more than ever before. Although Jackson generates much empathy for the beast, such emotions are strictly supplementary to the technological skill, as the vivid, almost sublime sensory impact of Jackson's digital hyperrealism facilitates our rousing itch for evermore ferocious spectacle.

Jackson's film already suggests a near future of 3-D. But the shock of Kong's meaty fist swiping out from the screen, millimetres from our noses, will soon pall; and the next phase in cinematic evolution, by which time gorillas will probably be extinct, will surely reside with full sensory participation. Perhaps some version of the translation of Andy Serkis from human to gorilla will be made available in virtual reality auditoria in which we will be wired up to entertainment machines for a hybrid experience. As an adjunct to military training usage, alongside the virtual porn, combat, and snuff film franchises that digital technology will inevitably give rise to, Kong will roar again. I imagine entering a Skull Island dome filled with Kong-burger kiosks and surround-screen booths, in which I'll plug in and become Kong for fifteen minutes, venting my rage, my anguished tantrums; finally finding out how Kong feels, putting on his knowledge with his power, no doubt relieved and stupefied.

Five Odes

MICHAEL FOLEY

The Spring Ode

It's regime-change at last. Like a geriatric tyranny, winter's collapsed.
    The old man's stubble, frosty grass, shines sleek and green,
the black trees put out leaves and the nymphs return, teasing and fleet of foot.
    Already city blossoms are out – everywhere women's white limbs.
A ripple of shoulder blades – wings of a powerful bird shrouded in silk.
    Forearm hairs curving in unison – reeds in the wind on
a sunny dune. Now the heavy extinguishers are propping open office doors
    and playful zephyrs tease the cappuccino froth on
pavement tables once more, thawing deep-frozen hearts and releasing desires.
    The chorus of needs when a tyranny falls! Every
search engine's key words are 'south', 'sun' and 'sex'. But ah, you who get there
    to bask on the scarce loungers, cocktails and leisurewear
matching in splendour the zinnias poolside, offer a sacrifice to your inscrutable
    Gods, for the ocean that looks so calm discontentedly flexes,
awaiting commitment, direction, momentum, the upsurge that sweeps all before it
    and wherever you've flown, however distant and warm,
hungry ghosts and icy nothingness are near . . . while diversity-celebrating Death
    sweeps with equal disdain past the gangsters of shanty towns
and the suited security in the five-star hotels . . . then creeps up silently behind
    to clap hot eyes with hands of bone and cackle: *Guess who?*

The Yellow Nib, Vol. 2, 2006, pp. 35–39
© Michael Foley

Ode to Glory

You aspire to be an iron man, Lucullus, laconic, proud, keenly observant
– but one of the things you'll observe is that the weak have all the fun.
And this strength of yours? Snobbery, stinginess, bullying. Is it strong
to make Lydia's eye make-up run? No, my friend. The wise Gods have
granted us slack time for loafing, indulgences, dreaming, bad taste
     – and woe to any too pure to avail.

Now that sleet, hail and face-numbing east winds abate, it is good
to go forth again. The deep-frozen city succumbs to a light caress.
Even bronze warriors soften a bit. So no scowls, Lucullus. Never
saturnine on Saturday. Stroll out with Lydia from boutique to boutique,
assessing the spring stock and waiting benignly by changing rooms.
     The Gods may reward with enchantment

– a white flash of nymphs. Or reward yourself with coffee and carrot cake,
and when the light becomes tender and intimate, the neon soft in oyster grey
ashimmer with immanence, so you feel something sensitive is trying
to communicate, the Gods are beseeching you, Lucullus, to see the old bar
with the 2-for-1 Happy Hour deal and beyond it the cheap little restaurant
     where you can bring your own wine.

Then even the Gods can do no more. Only you can recognise that what you so
impatiently dismissed is the miracle – to kindle yearning in a woman's eyes.
For muscled supermen of stadium and battle never glory more sublime
than when, with one of those twisted grins that stir her so, you pass a remark,
low and lewd, and she laughs and bends as though in pain over the table top:
     Oh God I'm going all funny downstairs.

The Born-Again Ode

As we dream at our supermarket trolley helms, Postumus,
    the desultory middle years pass in a flash.
Everything slows gently down – except time . . . alas!
    Recklessly speeding years know no restraint.

So it's vain to pack your trolley with organic fruit, seedless grapes
    (made for an age that wants flesh but not pips),
cool fragrant Gala melon, erubescent mangoes of marvellous heft,
    rugged pineapple – warrior's headdress and head.

Or tomato juice for prostate care or oily fish, omega-3-fatty-acid-rich,
    to open up lanes to your silt-threatened heart.
That will occlude and shrink anyway. (We would like to like more people
    more . . . but will probably like fewer less.)

Flare, gutter, snuff – that's the sum of it. Scatter my ash at least!
    Never the urn on the mantelpiece. Up and away
to the four winds on some gusty day, discontented, capricious
    and grey as this life we're so loath to depart.

Everything's reborn – though downwards – your manuscripts not under glass
    but recycled as lavatory roll, and your library,
hand-chosen, pampered (no dog ear, cracked spine or stained page),
    sharing charity-shop shelves with diet books.

Likewise your jazz CDs, many rare, hunted for years, *revered* . . . in among
    film themes and (*God forbid*) soul, while your wine rack
of Sancerre and Pinot Noir's glugged by some boor with no conception of
    'vibrant astringency' or 'liquorice notes'.

And as your wandering dust seeks a resting place, Phyllida too, yes she too,
    will be born again (who now has time to mourn,
fire-engine red is the new black), slimmed down and surgically tightened up
    before hitting town with a painted mouth ready to suck.

Ode to *It*

When it's good nothing's better. When it's bad nothing's worse. Alas, mostly
It's bad. As we know to our cost, Iccius. And also capricious, contrarian, false.
Maddening . . . but sublime. More exciting than sex. More obsessive than sport.
More addictive than smack – one or two easy youthful hits hook you for life.
But impervious to supplication, application, style – a diviner-resistant divine
That you can never recall how you summoned last time (and even if you could
The trick wouldn't work twice) or can ever be sure of enticing again, however
Solemn the rites or ingenious the ruse (such as trying to come upon it unawares,
Surprise the surprise). Nor will pattern analysis offer clues – nothing for years
. . . Then a *deluge*. And no pulling rank. Everyone has to wait . . . and then wait
Another age. Neophyte and high priest alike in abasement. And the thing itself
Inscrutably strange. The best always looks as though *anyone* could do it . . .
A gift from the blue . . . or, more likely, the grey . . . on some ordinary day when
You've duties and chores . . . but you'd shirk, cheat and lie, pimp your mother
For this. Nothing else will suffice. All is boredom when no lightning strikes.
And when it does nothing else can come near. The celebrity needs applause.
This is its own reward – feet mired in squalor but head lost among the stars.

The Reconciliation Ode

You, Lucullus, would like me to write rants, defiant, fierce, rhythmically grand,
compound-adjective-rich . . . and insouciantly hurl them at the implacable Gods
      but instead I'm at my desk with a self-appraisal form.
Note Achievements of This Year: Survived. *Set Objectives for Next Year*: Much
      more of the same. *Additional Comments*: Reconciled.

A *rapprochement*, late, strange and benign. Now I feel not apart, but a part of it
– that nothing's redundant, Lucullus (except TV chefs), that even my violations
      celebrate oneness (I open a Brie without tearing the paper,
peel a tangerine in one fluent spiral of zest) . . . and that even the husks of
      extinguished heresiarchs nourish old mother earth.

So I like to sit on at my desk as light fades . . . buildings empty . . . and across in
the Ethnic Small Business Unit the big sofa, royal blue, in the reception area
      takes on a lurid intensity, the water cooler rears
its bulk, strong and occult, and in the shadowy depths, right away at the back,
      an unattended computer solipsistically glows.

Thirty-three Years On: Ingeborg Bachmann, Poet, Novelist, Philosopher, Bohemian

MARY O'DONNELL

An essay and five translations

Ingeborg Bachmann once wrote that love triumphs, and death too, because death's triumph is time itself, and yet more time. When her own death came, it was through fire. Based then in Rome and absorbed by work on a prose trilogy (one novel of which, *Malina*, was published during her life), she took some tranquillisers on the night of 26 September 1973, determined to sleep. She got into bed and lit a cigarette. When she awoke, her night-clothes were on fire. She stumbled to the shower and managed to extinguish the flames, then ran the bathwater to further cool the burns. Only then did she phone a friend. The doctors at the Sant' Eugenio clinic could not save her. Forty per cent of the writer's skin had been burned and she died on 17 October 1973.

Only three months earlier she had spoken warmly in an interview for ORF Wien about the country in which she was to die, on the one hand recognising herself as an outsider despite having lived there for many years, but at the same time acknowledging the different ways in which she had experienced the country.

> I believe I know Italy's problems quite well by now, and it's not an identification on my part so much as an empathetic thinking and doing with these people who speak spontaneously and very openly with me and for whom something they still call a class war exists. For the workers are naturally very intelligent here. They know who they are, they know what they have to do and they have an inordinately

The Yellow Nib, Vol. 2, 2006, pp. 40–56

strong consciousness of that which is not possible and that which is. And I love these people. The reason I love Italy has nothing to do with its beauties, *but because I have grasped why and for what this people struggles* [my italics].

Ingeborg Bachmann was one of the few German women writers, apart from Christa Wolf, who became established as an important European writer in the latter half of the twentieth century. Born in the Austrian town of Klagenfurt in 1926, the daughter of a grammar-school teacher, her earliest memories were coloured by her experience of the German occupation of her homeland, and the devastation which ensued. She studied philosophy, psychology and germanistics at Innsbruck, Graz and Vienna, and in 1950 completed a doctoral thesis on Heidegger, but poetry, not philosophy, became the genre for which she was eventually celebrated. By 1953 she was one of the talented younger women who graced the largely masculine scene of the Gruppe 47 writers' association, winning in that year the influential Gruppe 47 poetry prize.[1] Between then and her death in 1973, she received many more awards for her work, including the Bremen Literature Prize and the Georg Büchner Prize.

Apart from poetry, Bachmann wrote radio plays dating back to the time when she worked for the Viennese radio station Rot/Weiss/Rot. Her prose, including many fragments, consists of an inexhaustible range of variations on established themes. When she was awarded the Hörspielpreis der Kriegsblinden, a radio drama award named in honour of the war-blind, in 1959, she referred publicly to hidden pain as an inherent aspect of human nature which, when recognised, activates our instinct to advance towards perfection in every sphere of experience. It is this world of values about which – unlike Wittgenstein's view in the *Tractatus* – the writer is free to articulate, and to which Ingeborg Bachmann attuned her artistic and aesthetic energies throughout her short life.

Influenced by Wittgenstein and Robert Musil, as well as the post-war poet Paul Celan (whom she first met in Vienna at the end of 1947), she displayed a critical attitude to language and tradition, with major themes in her poetry springing from her experience of the occupation of Austria in 1938 when she was twelve years old, the horrors of the war and the Holocaust itself. Beyond this, and deriving from it, lay her sense that history was always doomed to self-replicate. The warning 'Es kommen härtere Tage' ('Harder times are ahead') from the title poem of the collection Die gestundete Zeit (Time-lapse) demonstrates this intensity of feeling, although the poem is both spare and restrained. She implies rather than exhorts, as in 'Holz und Späne' ('Wood and Splinters'). The title poem of her second collection, Anrufung des Großen Bären (Invoking the Great Bear, 1956) denounces the misuse of power inherent in any organised ideology. Apart from the biblical and mythological connotations of the sign of the Great Bear, it was also used by Simone Weil (as 'das Grosse Tier') and Bachmann draws attention to this link in her 1955 essay on the philosopher.

What follows is part of an interview with Munich-based freelance journalist, producer and editor Joachim von Bernstorff on 26 March 1956. Fifty years on, Bachmann's views on the lyric poem and the question of how poetic language expands from the groundwork of the past seem remarkably fresh and applicable to the poetry of today.

BERNSTORFF: Do you believe that the contemporary poem still holds the potential to be taken up by the world around us, which is defined by rationality and technology, at least here in northern Europe? And, further-more, might not the lyric be overwhelmed by human haste itself, when people have no time to listen, to the extent that even poets or potential poets will be prevented from making any sustained poetic statement?

BACHMANN: They will not be prevented, they will never be prevented from achieving a poetic statement, especially if they have something to say, and furthermore their own time will not prevent them from speaking out, but will demand it, every generation demands a statement. Nonetheless, the question must naturally be asked again: 'What purpose have poets in needy times?' More accurately the question should be 'What purpose has poetry [my italics] in needy times?' That's a question in the spirit of Hölderlin. You can see that it was raised very early indeed.

BERNSTORFF: Did Hölderlin write that in his prose . . .?

BACHMANN: No, it's from his elegy 'Bread and Wine'.

BERNSTORFF: So the topic has always existed, and from the poetic or lyrical standpoint each period must somehow be interrogated . . . You also state that our time is no less unworthy than other times. But I spoke earlier of how the rational holds particular dangers for the poetic. On the other hand it offers something outrageously liberating. And that makes me think that in the modern poetry, and also in your own poetry, the rational impulse plays a particular role, and that old images, metaphors and also ideas such as those we're accustomed to from the lyric poets of the past are somehow undone and changed through this rational way of thinking?

BACHMANN: Yes, they are changed. To put it this way: if you compare language to a town, then there's always an old town centre, and newer areas of the town are joined on, and finally the filling stations and suburban streets, and the town periphery which appears so revolting in comparison to the old centre; but even so it all belongs together and comprises the town of today.

BERNSTORFF: That's a lovely image, which brings me to my second question. Many of us naturally find the old town centres at their most beautiful in medieval towns like Rothenburg or Nuremberg, and that which is outside – you've already said it yourself – appears naked and hateful, too expedient; but such romanticising is surely a failure and also an inhibitor, if one is to comprehend the contemporary, or is to understand our own time and our own poetry?

BACHMANN: It's an inhibitor for many people.

BERNSTORFF: Can you name a few poets, or even a poem, in which the contemporary is brought to full expression?

BACHMANN: Perhaps I can mention a couple of the younger German poets whom I believe express this best, say Günther Eich or Paul Celan.

BERNSTORFF: I'd like to return to something again, your image of the old town. Many would say: these old lyric poems, the poems of years gone by, the romantic poems . . .

BACHMANN: Can I interrupt here . . . I'm sorry, but what I mean is that we should compare the poems, the old poems, with the ancient heart of the town. Language itself, I believe, is like a town, and new words are just grafted onto it, and the old poems are made from the old linguistic material, the newer from both old and new. Some are made solely from the new.

BERNSTORFF: You mean that the vocabulary of technology, of modern civilisation, is part of the newer poetry? That's true, very many words now exist which were not there earlier. But what about those who believe that the older poetry belongs in a museum? That it has something to say to us, that we find it beautiful, just like old art in old museums, but that these ancient poetries cannot speak to us immediately. That's what a small circle of the so-called avant garde would say, but surely that's a misunderstanding?

BACHMANN: Yes, it's a misunderstanding. The modernity of a poem is something distinct from the presence of a poem, and I believe that the most wonderful old poems, or poems from older times, possess this presence . . .

By no means an 'easy' writer, the task of translating a selection of Ingeborg Bachmann's work began for me as far back as 1987, when I worked on five or six of the poems from *Anrufung des Großen Bären*. I felt automatically attracted to Bachmann's abstractions, to the fact that for her the concrete 'telling detail' – nowadays so unquestioned – seems not always to represent an essential characteristic of poetry. There is a melancholy and, sometimes in opposition to this, an elevated, heightened tone which works within the poetry and makes it a challenging proposition, not least because thematically she offers no obvious formulae, no codes for survival during our transient encounter with self and others in the world.

Ingeborg Bachmann was a bohemian.[2] Despite a solidly bourgeois belief in the totality of the individual and individual concerns, her life-long allegiance was to the value of two things – art and love. She was intolerant of anything less than perfection, the ideal, the absolute commitment, and her late poem 'Böhmen liegt am Meer' ('Bohemia is by the Sea', 1914) shows her to be

> [. . .] a bohemian, gypsy, owning nothing, keeping nothing,
> still negotiating the cantankerous sea, to catch sight
> of the land of my choosing.

The land of her choosing was something Bachmann constantly turned over. Widely travelled, and gradually in great demand both for interviews and as a reader and lecturer – though she refused to be drawn on her personal life – it was as if she entered each new country with the lens of her consciousness wide open, thus allowing the various preoccupations of a philosophical mind free rein to inspect and absorb what she found there. In an interview in June 1973 she voiced her ideas on the capacities of men and women as well as on the socialist debate that was to the fore in central Europe at the time. Having returned from Warsaw and a highly respectful discussion there with the journalist and writer Alicja Walecka-Kowalska, who had a special interest in Polish–German relations, here are some of Bachmann's thoughts unreined:

> Most women need a hope, something that has never been said to them before. I don't need it, I've known for a long time that they are capable of thinking exactly and as sharply as men. That they are just as capable, that they are even less conceited, that they are capable of greater achievements than men. That they have no need of sympathy and are capable of every sacrifice in order to do something. That was the doctrine the Poles conveyed to me. However, although I don't need to say this to myself, I wanted to say to other women: go to Poland and look at what Polish women are doing. And they are not unfeminine; on the contrary, they are perhaps the most womanly

women in the world. They really are women and despite that they do something and they do a lot, basically they do the best. And it's no joke . . . Who rules Poland? The women! But the truth, because I don't want to be unfair, isn't quite so. The truth is that the women and men there work together towards a future, with one another and not against one another. What so often prevails here [in Italy] has ceased to exist there. In Italy, in this land I love so greatly, which considers women to be inferior, where it's said that women have I don't know how many less grams of brain, that they cannot think. That is not true. Women can do just as much as men, they only need the chance . . .

Thirty-three years on, Bachmann's thoughts seem to be occupying the more elementary levels of debate on both the socialist and feminist experiments. They sound naive from today's perspective, where the great bands of 'isms' have been broken up, deconstructed, rearranged to accommodate shifting demographies, shifting cultural perspectives and the huge and ongoing polarisation that is occurring daily between the West – which has absorbed Bachmann's vital Poland in its EU skin – and the Middle East and East. Yet her rationale was perfectly sound. They are the instinctive thoughts of a thinking person of her time, and also the thoughts of someone who lived to some extent like an unattached male. The geographies of the interior and exterior belonged to her, were hers to explore. Like the language of poetry that she compared to an old town centre which is being constantly expanded under the influence of time, so too did her system of ideas expand as she absorbed the various 'graftings' of her own time.

I have not included her juvenilia in this selection. I suspect that Bachmann herself might not care for it very much in hindsight, although of course I cannot know this. The kernel of her work appears from 1948 onwards, when she finally sheds the excesses of the tragic-romantic posturing which characterised the earliest material and begins a committed exploration of the formal and structural aspects of poetry, gradually asserting an unstinting control even within the free verse work found alongside regular rhymed stanzas. She was a superb technician as well as a philosopher: living within a society which was not, by and large in those post-war years, anti-intellectual, this was not seen to be detrimental. If anything, her highly calibrated intellectual sweep informs the poetry and contributes to its challenge.

During her life, Bachmann's interest in music resulted in collaborations on a number of projects with the composer Hans Werner Henze, who was a close friend.[3] By the end of the 1950s, when she had written libretti for a ballet and an opera by Henze as well as produced a number of radio plays (with music by Henze), her work had undergone a critical transformation, and the nature of this reappraisal was reflected in her lectures at Frankfurt University.

Die gestundete Zeit fairly vibrates with absences, despite the often inhabited, even cluttered settings of some of the poems in the collection. Whether she is in England, Paris or Munich, Bachmann never loses sight of the possibility of 'harder times' ahead. The good is on loan, as it were, time has lapsed and very likely will recover from its comfortable, if transient, loss of form. She draws succour from the natural cycles, from seed spread ('Sterne im März' / 'The Stars in March'), from the sight of rivers, rain and light, recognising all the time that history may have 'booked us a grave, / from which there is no resurrection'.

At times, Bachmann creates apocalyptic scenarios, as in the poem 'Vision', which announces

> When these ships come ashore . . .
> No, not ashore!
> We shall die like the net-hauled fish
> that rock around them on the widening swell
> to thousandfold corpses!

There can be little doubt that the early experience of invasion and Fascism had long-term consequences for Bachmann's vision of life and for her writing. A sense of impending doom hovers over much of the poetry, disaster has either happened or is about to, and the individual is faced with one choice only: survival. This preoccupation with Fascism and tyranny also found its place in her fiction, especially in the novel *Malina* (1971), which she declared was autobiographical, though not in the conventional sense of that word. She described it instead in an interview with Veit Mölder in March 1971 as 'eine geistige, imaginäre Autobiographie' ('an intellectual, imaginary autobiography'). The intriguing thing about this novel is that two of the 'characters' are one and the same person. Malina is a man, in love with Ivan. But the narrating female 'Ich', who initially appears to be a separate character, is actually Malina's doppelgänger, and he hers. This male and female tension continues throughout, and Bachmann's variation on the doppelgänger motif is simply that the Ich (feminine) has a masculine opposite (Malina).

When the book was published in Italy, Bachmann was asked if the novel's second chapter referred to Fascistic incidents in her by now adopted city. She replied that it was written much earlier, that she had long considered the origins of Fascism.

It does not begin with the first bombs that are written about in every newspaper. It begins in the relations between people. Fascism is the first [element] in the connection between a man and a woman, and I've tried to say, in this chapter, that this society is always at war. There is no war and peace, only war. Relations between the man and the woman are not problematic for the first time today. They must always have been so, because otherwise we would not have so many books, from the Bible on, to the great literatures of every country, with so much to say about the matter. Today, the situation is obviously something different, because the majority of women work, are independent and yet not independent. This has not been a problem for me. I have always known from the outset that I was opposed to marriage, to every legal bind. Although that doesn't exclude the possibility that relations which are not legal and binding can be just as tragic and horrific as those which are legal. And Italian women workers are opposing marriage for the first time, and fighting for their freedom . . . Marriage is an impossible institution. It is impossible for a woman who works and who thinks and who wants something.

Throughout Bachmann's work, absences within the multiplicities of human experience are recognised, and despite that recognition comes the knowledge that survival can only happen when risk is taken: risk in living, in writing, in loving, in not leaning into the (in its own way) possibly commendable but ultimately corrupting peace of the bourgeois. Bachmann brings us tasty and testy words: salt and bread, a storm of roses, psalms, images of the shore and the land, of fish and knives and waves cut by knives, of skeletons and earthquakes, of thickets and constellations, of treacherous lovers with whom one inhabits a 'fog-land'. All the time, the ceaseless quest for enlightenment, which, for Bachmann, is experienced through love and art, through the guiding aesthetic principle. Truth, she warns in 'Was wahr ist' ('Truth') is difficult. It does not guarantee the space one imagines. It might – she suggests – ultimately lead towards the unknown exit point within one's existential prison. Either way, one is compelled to *look* in poems which incorporate elements of an imagined exotic 'south' ('Lieder von einer Insel' / 'Songs from an Island') with something much chillier, withdrawn and internalised. Bachmann stands as witness to many things not literally named but suggested and anticipated in the apocalyptic visions of fire and deluge, of flight from the enemy and asylum (always temporary) in other restive landscapes.

SOURCES

Ingeborg Bachmann, *Sämtliche Gedichte* (Piper Verlag, 1978)
Ingeborg Bachmann, *Wir müssen wahre Sätze finden: Gespräche und Interviews*
    (Piper Verlag, 1991)
Ingeborg Bachmann, *Malina* (Suhrkamp Taschenbuch Verlag, 1980)

A shorter version of this essay was published in *Poetry Ireland Review*, Winter 2004

NOTES
1   Becoming, some would argue, subsequently fashioned into an icon of feminine poetic
    sensibility.
2   'At best,' she said in one of her lectures when she held the University of Frankfurt's first
    Chair of Poetry in the winter semester of 1959/60, 'the poet can succeed in two ways: by
    representing his time, and by presenting something, the time for which has not yet
    come.'
3   Later involved with Swiss dramatist Max Frisch, Bachmann moved between Rome and
    Zurich from 1958 to 1962. Frisch went on to publicise their relationship in an
    autobiographical story which emphasised minutiae rather than fully representing
    Bachmann.

Freight

Summer's great cargo is loaded,
the sun-freight lies ready in the dock,
even if a gull cries and plunges behind you.
Summer's great cargo is loaded.

The sun-freight lies ready in the dock,
the smiles of lemurs are unveiled
on the lips of those on the galley.
The sun-freight lies ready in the dock.

Even if a gull cries and plunges behind you,
the command to go down comes from the West;
wide-eyed, you'll drown in light nonetheless,
even if a gull cries and plunges behind you.

Bohemia is by the Sea

If the houses hereabouts are primitive, I'll step into one.
If the bridges are sound, I'll seek high ground.
If love's pain is lost to all time, I'll gladly lose it here.

If I am not the one, then one as good as me.
If my boundaries are pushed back, so be it.
If Bohemia is by the sea, I'll believe again
                in seas.
Yet believing in the sea, I still hanker for land.

If I am the one, then so is everyone, as much as me.
I desire nothing more for myself. I wish to perish.

To perish – meaning by the sea, I'll find Bohemia there again.
Set to perish, I awaken calm.
Knowing the fundamentals, I remain unforsaken.

Come here, you Bohemians, sea-farers, harbour whores
                and unanchored
ships. Don't strive for the Bohemian, you Illyrians, Veronese,
and Venetians. Perform the comedies that make us laugh

And weep. And stray a hundred times,
as I have done and never stood trial,
but I have been tested, time and again,

Just as Bohemia stood trial and one fine day
was pardoned by the sea and now lies by the water.

I am on the verge of utterance, and another country,
on the verge, however slightly, but
> more and more towards everything,

a bohemian, a gypsy, owning nothing, keeping nothing,
still negotiating the cantankerous sea, to catch sight
> of the land of my choosing.

Leaving England

Silent land, I have scarcely stepped
on your soil, disturbed a stone,
I was raised so high above your heaven,
so set on clouds, vapour and distant things,
that I left nearly as soon
as I dropped anchor.

You sealed my eyes
with sea-breath and oak leaves,
you kept the grasses plump,
watered by my tears;
loosed from my dreams,
suns ventured out,
yet everything fled,
once your day began.
Everything was unsaid.

Great grey birds fluttered through
the streets, banishing me.
Was I ever here?

I did not want to be seen.
My eyes are open.
Sea-breath and oak leaves?
Beneath the sea-serpents
in your place, I see
how the land succumbs to my soul.

I have scarcely stepped on its soil.

Invoking the Great Bear

Great Bear, come down, shaggy night,
cloud-pelted animal with ancient eyes,
starred eyes,
your glistening paws break
through the thicket with claws,
starred claws,
wary we cling to the hearth,
yet entranced by you, we distrust
your weary flanks and the sharp
half-stripped teeth,
ancient Bear.

A fir-cone: your human world.
The cone-scales: you.
I drive it, roll it
from the first forests
to the forests at the end,
snort at it, taste it in my mouth
and seize it with my paws.

Fear or fear not!
Pay to the beggar's pouch and spare
a kind word for the blind man,
that he may hold the bear to the leash.
And season the lamb well.

Could be, that this bear
rips himself loose, no longer menaces,
hunts the cones that fell from the firs,
the great, the winged,
that plunged from Paradise.

Enlighten Me, Love

Your hat rises softly, greets, waves in the wind,
your unadorned head bewitches the clouds,
your heart is doing its business elsewhere,
your mouth absorbs new languages.
The quivering grass spreads through the land,
Summer blows on starflowers, on and off,
gossamer-blinded you raise your face,
you laugh and weep and go to ruin,
what else could happen to you –

Enlighten me, love!

The peacock spreads his tail in solemn amazement,
the pigeon holds his feathered collar high,
brimful of cooing, the air expands,
the mallard shrieks, the whole countryside
takes its fill of wild honey, even in the formal park
each flower is hemmed with golden dust.

The fish flushes, overtakes the school
and rushes through grottoes to a coral bed,
the skittish scorpion dances to a tune of silver sand,
the beetle smells his glorious mate from afar;
had I his style I too would imagine
how wings shimmer beneath her armour,
and make my way to the distant strawberry patch!

Enlighten me, love!

Water can speak,
wave taking wave by the hand,
in the vineyard the grape swells, leaps and falls,
how guilelessly the snail forsakes its shell!

A stone knows how to soften another stone!

Enlighten me, love, about what I cannot explain:
Should I trade with ideas alone
during this short ghastly spell
and know nothing or do nothing lovable?
Must one think? Are we not missed?

You say: another mind depends on yours . . .
Enlighten me no more. I see the salamander
move through every fire.
No shudder drives him, and there is no agony.

Three Poems

NIALL McGRATH

Road Kill

A pad down the bank from the hedge
Leads my gaze to where this carcase lies;
Only the fox's bones remain,
Once verge grass grew through rotted flesh;
To be crushed into muck by a tractor's tyre
As the councilman mowed April growth.

Already a bloody splodge
On tarmac, the hedgehog's
Bristles glint in spring's
Clarity; uninteresting.

You'd imagine the pigeon would fly out of the way;
If I'd known, I'd have honked the horn, not just driven on;
It waddled, its back turned, oblivious to danger;
When the grille struck its head – an eruption of feathers.

The Yellow Nib, Vol. 2, 2006, pp. 57–60
© Niall McGrath

The Accordionists

My father-in-law gigged Carnegie and the Albert halls,
My father ceilied in Loanends Orange Hall.

On the living room wall, with Pat Boone in cowboy hat,
Alongside President McAleese, a bronze accordionist.

A video captures Paddy's Galloglass arrangements,
Late Late Show footage, trad entertainment.

Dad's mate upturned a tea-chest as drums,
Stour rose to their rustic thrums;

The youth of Ireland, in more innocent times,
North and South romanced to self-taught rhythms.

When confirming bookings for each night,
'No ham' was the main clause Sheila'd write.

Sunday Morning in the Garden of Eden

Fred Wilson is mowing his lawn, disturbing
The peace of everyone who's had a couple,
Like Frank next door, whose beds are perturbing
Thanks to all the weeds that rule.

Eva and Jules are heading to Yum-yums
For cappuccino and croissants and a dose of tabloids.
Mr Kirk, sixty-six, leers at their bums,
Retires upstairs to cream his haemorrhoids.

Rocky Love is on his knees painting
Flowerboxes either side of the front door;
He pauses to notice, opposite, a panting
Alasdair as he draws a curtain, chest bare:

Audrey is pumping a swollen breast
With a squeaking machine. At the shop later,
Billy admonishes Al for doing *that*
On the Sabbath: his righteous neighbour.

Billy returns to sit in the parlour
With his *Sunday Mail*, meanwhile Gwen
Is preparing chicken, sneaks a gin
As hubby rants about today's social squalor.

Peter is in his loft conversion,
An amateur studio, getting to grips
With the intricacies of his latest creation,
Re-oiling his model's nips.

His subject, single mum Sally, at thirty-eight,
Is in the throes of an argument with her son,
Who doesn't want to rise from his pit
For Sunday School now he's a surly teen.

She relents, so Luke wanders by the river,
His bitch loose, being full of reverie,
Eyes, ears and nose sparking with the electricity,
Rapt in the atmosphere generated by nature;

Passes, unknowingly, Trudy and Eric
Snuggled in the bushes, shooing away the dog
That tried to sniff his restrained dick,
Rudely interrupted their surreptitious snog.

Jessie scampers with a momentary whine
From gorse clumps to rabbit holes,
Destroys Luke's ecstasy when she mauls
A rag of rotting fur and bone.

Returning to the estate, Luke bobs on
As Fred mops his brow beneath a high sun,
Merely nods when the old geezer speaks,
Winces when the back door squeaks

And his mum calls out, while the TV titillates
With some reality show. Above the copse,
Bells clang on the stillness
Of another Sunday as the snake of time oscillates.

Time, Fashion, Terror
The Prose of Stéphane Mallarmé

PATRICK McGUINNESS

An essay and a poem

Refining Mallarmé at last destroyed
Flesh, passion and their consequent confusions;
His poetry continued in a void
Where only furniture could have illusions.

THOM GUNN, 'Readings from the French'

No, he would not blow up the world; he would put it in parentheses

JEAN-PAUL SARTRE, Mallarmé

Whatever we may think of when we hear the name Stéphane Mallarmé, it's not likely to be bombs, fashion magazines or politics. The Mallarmé we know is the poet who sought the 'Orphic explanation of the world', the 'Prince des poètes' (an elected position in fin-de-siècle Paris) for whom everything 'exist[ed] to finish up in a beautiful book'. We know the poems too, just as we know the Mallarmé we've been taught about: denizen of the ivory tower, poet of absence, loss, sterility; the poet in whose work language mourns what it perhaps never had, only to conjure it imperiously back into presence as a looking-glass world of double negatives. Mallarmé is traditionally called a poet of suggestion, but he is not, like Paul Verlaine, a poet of the mellifluous, quivering, *indécis*. Most of the other Symbolists are poets of porous borders, pastel shades and blurred outlines. Mallarmé is the poet of the crystalline and the prismatic; his poems are like cut diamonds catching the light – in his

The Yellow Nib, Vol. 2, 2006, pp. 61–76

own analogy, the poem is the jewel, the faceted stone, and reading the light that runs and flickers and plays over it.

A Mallarmé poem does not hesitate between meanings – it forces the reader to do so, something entirely different. And because no reader can hesitate indefinitely, Mallarmé's poems may equally well be read as exercises in enforced decision-making. That contrast in his work between the assertiveness of the syntax (powerful driving verbs, imperious assertions, dramatic parentheses) and the ambiguity, often the absence, of the poem's 'subject', is what gives us that sense, at once, of compression and emptiness, as if we were being manhandled across a void. No reader of his poems can fail to register the imbrications of his syntax, his clausal jugglings and suspensions. Single sentences can last one, two, three stanzas; sometimes whole poems. The poem's syntax is all transition, pressing ahead, tumbling over the rhyme that for a moment stalls it, then revving back up into another assault on its own end, an end which, at the same time, it expertly defers. The subject or object of a Mallarméan sentence is often the last element to come into view. To reach it, we must conjure up interpretations that are provisional, but necessary to keep us moving along. When the poem's end is reached, these are not cancelled out. A poem (and a Mallarmé poem especially) is not just what it means; it is the product of its discarded meanings clamouring behind us, the way our own echoes, voices left along the past, help orientate us in the present. Mallarmé's poems are good at using poetry's waste products, high-efficiency machines that draw their aborted interpretations and investigative dead ends back into themselves. Even the blank page, as he wrote in the preface to *Un Coup de Dés* (*A Throw of the Dice*), 'assumes significance'.

Mallarmé's poetry may be difficult, but it's his prose that really baffles. He revised his poems to make them more difficult, often by removing punctuation, while at the same time intensifying the semantic rush that punctuation would traditionally have helped pace. In his prose it is the opposite, though difficulty remains the end result. Mallarmé's prose writings, especially his late pieces, are obsessively punctuated. His sentences are fiendishly long, full of leaps ahead and castings back, and peppered with idiosyncratic punctuation marks. He has a particular affection for anything that helps defer and suspend the line's unfolding. Commas and parentheses are often asymmetrically used, while colons and semi-colons exist less to isolate semantic events than to give the sentence a quick breather before it propels itself forward into (or at) the next tangent. He is fond too of the dash – a *point d'illumination* he calls it – and of marks that introduce hesitations, delays, that inject intervals; but also that provoke sudden leaps back and forth and sideways in the reading process. His sentences are really several sentences in one, braided together, interjecting into each other's propositions, like radio frequencies where different stations break into and out of our hearing.

In 'Mystery in Letters' (1896) Mallarmé has something to say about how he understands the sentence to function:

> What linchpin do I understand there to be, amid these contrasts, for understanding? There must be a guarantee –
>
> Syntax –
>
> Not, simply, its spontaneous tricks, as found in the easeful movements of conversation; although artifice can persuade by its address. [. . .] A sudden lofty play of wingbeats can be mirrored too: whoever leads in this game discovers that an extraordinary adaptation has taken place between structure, in its limpidity, and the primeval wrath of logic. A babbling – that is how the sentence seems, though here held in check by the insertion of parenthetical matter – proliferates, and is organised and transported to some higher equilibrium, a planned interplay of inversions.

This is Mallarméan prose defined: the play-off between the sentence's natural will towards limpidity and the 'primeval wrath of logic'; the 'planned interplay of inversions'; the holding aloft and *holding up* of 'parenthetical matter'. It is not a homogenising, linear whole but a mesh of differently calibrated advances, a set of different clausal time-zones all unfolding at different paces, but also driving towards a common end.

The globe was cut into time zones in the 1880s, and it may not be too fanciful to think of a Mallarméan sentence as a microcosm of a world in which it can be night and day at the same time, midnight and midday. He talked of the '*éspacement de la lecture*', the 'spacing out of reading', and we can see his prose as an attempt to create something like a musical sense of the line. The poems read like extraordinary efforts at compression and purification; the prose, on the contrary, seems like a perpetual effort at incorporation and prolongation. Why? Grand definitions of the differences between prose and poetry often sound stupid or self-serving, but it is worth having a go at one here, if only to give someone else the chance to contradict it. It is possible to see poetry, lyric poetry especially, and in the nineteenth century most of all, as the form that strives to escape time and transcend temporality. Lyric's vertical obsession (Baudelaire's 'azur', for instance) contrasts with prose's sense of horizontal progress (the nineteenth-century 'Realist' novel for instance). Mallarmé's poems tend to be situated in aftermaths: a room has been empty, a song has stopped (or never been sung), someone is dead. Masking the stillness of these scenes is a language of pure, driving activity. Punctuation, we could say, is time deployed across syntax, and the poems do not just try to exit time in their subject matter, but to abolish time's enforcers – punctuation marks. Perhaps in this specific sense we can speak of Mallarmé's poetry locating itself outside time's constraints, all the while retaining a strong dose of semantic density and dynamism. In his prose, however, he seeks the opposite: to inhabit time – or, we could say, to have even more of it! But this is on his own terms: time as interval, time as suspension, time as pre-emption and prolepsis, time as flashback and déjà-vu, rather than what we could call the 'consensus-time' of straightforward linearity.

Mallarmé's view of time is not a standard one, and he makes gnomic statements about it. 'The future is only what should have happened sooner, or near the origin,' he declares – an extraordinary statement in an age polarised between those two unquestioningly linear paradigms: a belief in progress and an obsession with decline and decadence. Nothing Mallarmé says or writes suggests that he believes in either of these opposing but connected views, summarised, poetically speaking, by his predecessors Victor Hugo and Charles Baudelaire. For Hugo, progress is the present directed by the future. For Baudelaire, progress is a myth: the future is just more of the same, but less. In 'Restrained Action', Mallarmé writes: 'There is no present, no – a present does not exist', and adds: 'Ill-informed the one who would announce himself his own contemporary.' In his famous essay 'Crise de Vers' (1895), he claims that poetic history is a matter not of progress but of intermittences, jumps and lapses, breakdowns and fusions – crises, in fact. In 'Catholicism', he writes: 'Everything is interrupted, effectively, in history, with a minimum of transfusion.' His view of history is mirrored on the micro-level in the sentence: lulls and flashes, prolepses and analepses, pauses and accelerations. For Mallarmé, time is crisis.

Critics have been wary of engaging with Mallarmé's prose, and even his many commentators in French have tended (with a few exceptions) to give it a wide berth. But it is essential to Mallarmé. As well as being one of the great correspondents of the period, he wrote political and fashion journalism, opinion pieces on current affairs (bank collapses, the Panama canal, the *Expositions universelles*), as well as literary criticism and theatre reviews. He accepted the job of theatre critic for *La Revue Indépendante* on condition that he could write his reviews without seeing the play, telling the editor that 'sometimes just the programme read at the fireside will be enough'. The editor accepted, such was the prestige of Mallarmé in prose. It was a lucky decision: Mallarmé has left us a remarkable body of theatre theory. But one of the least studied aspects of Mallarmé's already understudied prose is his engagement in politics, and, more precisely, the radical and violent political dramas of his time.

'Destruction was my Beatrice'
Poetry and Terror

'*La Déstruction fut ma Béatrice*' wrote Mallarmé: 'Destruction was my Beatrice'. This glittering line was a favourite of Guy Debord, the situationist leader and author of *The Society of the Spectacle*, who quotes it in the opening of his autobiographical book *Panégyrique*.

You can tell a lot about poets from their prefixes. The single syllable of pre-emptive erasure, *dé-*, is Mallarmé's shortest and most resonant word, from his earliest sonnets to his great last poem, *Un Coup de dés Jamais n'Abolira le Hasard* (*A Throw of the Dice Will Never Abolish Chance*, 1897) – a throw of the dice (*dés*), yes, but also a throw of the negative prefix (*dé-*), a handful of undoing. Victor Hugo, the poet of plenitude and excess, is characterised by an abundance of *sur*-s, his poetry powered by prefixes of bursting and brimming over, of torrential eloquence, fearsome appetites and visionary dynamism. Hugo's great word is 'surnaturalisme', for which he shares a fondness with another prefix-driven poet, Baudelaire. In Baudelaire the range is broader: there is *sur-* and there is *mal-* and there is *dé-*, but, as in *Painter of Modern Life*, the '*déformation sublime de la nature*' is redeemed by what immediately (and causally) follows it: a '*réformation de la nature*'. Hugo accumulates and adds, Baudelaire dismantles and rebuilds, but only Mallarmé abolishes and undoes.

In April 1894, at the height of the anarchist bombings, Henri de Régnier recalls Mallarmé saying: 'Only one person has the right to be an anarchist: me, the poet, because only I make a product that society doesn't want, in exchange for which it gives me nothing to live on.' Superfluity in social and economic terms (joblessness, hopelessness, poverty, etc.) is one of the causes of revolutionary action. Mallarmé, from the comfort of his Rue de Rome flat, suggests the same applies to poets. Dangerous talk, certainly, and more combative than in 1891 when he declared in an interview that 'the case of the poet, in this society which does not permit him to make a living, is analogous to the case of someone isolating themselves to carve their own tomb'. On the one hand it is disproportionate and grandiose for a poet (and one little read even by other poets – we forget that the cult of Mallarmé was a sub-section of the sub-section that was poetry at the time) to lay claim to such extreme rhetoric. On the other, it had been festering throughout the nineteenth century. Baudelaire, heir to the romantics, knew it already: poetry's irrelevance became its liberty. Only the irrelevant are truly free, and Baudelaire's fantasies of flight must be seen in the context not just of traditional escapism but of poetry without the ballast of readership, working in a void and so idealising its void as azure. His predecessors, Alfred de Vigny, Alphonse de Lamartine and Hugo, had all been politicians and deputies, public figures and legislators, as well as writers with an organic audience. Baudelaire and Mallarmé's grand claims about poetry as an absolute are as much defiant retreats from the public sphere as they are professions of faith in their art. Mallarmé in fact never stops fantasising about a society in which politics and poetry are joined together, and his prose contains many intimations of what such a society might be: egalitarian, certainly, but also a cult of art; atheistic, but with a sense of ritual and ceremony. Aside from these improbable fantasies there are more nuanced comments, such as the one that comes at the end of 'Music and Letters', where he claims that the modern state is 'what a necropolis is in relation to the paradise it evaporates'. He goes on:

> voting, even for oneself, is not enough, as compared to the expansion of a hymn with trumpet accompaniment which intimates the happiness of pronouncing no name; nor does any uprising sufficiently wrap you round with the storm needed to rain down, to blend with the world, and to be reborn as a hero.

This seems an explicit rejection of the two available means of envisaging political action: democracy and revolution. But more specifically, it is a rejection of both the cult of the individual (even voting for oneself is not enough) and the cult of collective action (since it does not genuinely meld the individual with the world).

Earlier in the same essay, first given as a talk in Oxford and Cambridge in 1894, Mallarmé makes what must have been an extraordinary statement. Invited to talk about poetry and music, he in fact spends much of the lecture discussing politics, suffrage and – sandwiched between a paragraph on nature and a paragraph on free verse – bombs. One of his lecture's running metaphors has been light and illumination, and he invokes it again in this audacious paragraph:

> Missiles, their explosions illuminating parliaments with a summary light [*une lueur sommaire*], but maiming curious passers-by, in ways that arouse great pity, would still interest me because of their light – were it not that their lesson is so brief that it allows lawmakers to claim a definitive lack of understanding; but I criticise them for adding bullets and nails to that light.

The 'missiles' are a reference to the attacks by Max Nordau, author of *Degeneration* (1892), a book which accuses Mallarmé of perpetrating a 'bubble economy' of poetry, and describes the Symbolists as a criminal class diverted from direct action by their propensity for literature. Such ideas were not just insults, but seriously held: bubble economies created paper companies which didn't exist or which produced no goods; Symbolism called for readerly investment in poems that had no meanings. Nordau had also said that the literary avant-garde of the fin de siècle was simply a criminal class that could write – the same impulses that led to Symbolist poetry led, in illiterate men and women, to theft, erotomania and terrorism (he described Verlaine, for instance, as a 'mongoloid', a 'criminal' and a 'graphomaniac').

Taking up Nordau's metaphorical thread connecting poetry to politics and economics, Mallarmé deftly moves from the metaphorical missile to the real, literal missiles, alluding to the bombing of the French Chamber of Deputies the previous year by anarchist Emile Henry. This idea of explosive revelation, of the terrorist act as both meaningless and revelatory, gratuitous yet full of significance, is as provocative now as it would have been then. Mallarmé suggests – this is the age *par excellence* of propaganda by the deed – that bombs are fine if they illuminate (we think of Mallarmé's dashes, or 'points of illumination'), but not if they contain nails and bullets. This is hardly a condemnation of terror – in the next paragraph he calls terror 'the incoherence with which the street assails whomsoever hoards extreme riches' – but it is an attempt to match poetic and political justifications.

One Mallarmé text where political motifs, one could say motifs of terrorism, are explicitly counterpointed with motifs of high art is his short essay on fellow poet Laurent Tailhade, wounded in the anarchist bombing of the Restaurant Foyot in February 1894:

So much noise detonated . . .
The newspapers almost disfigured him.

The insult reduced to the chance event of the sinister flowerpot –
none would contain your majestic stalk, imagination, that is the

meaning attributable to the brute *fait divers* – this friend will emerge marked, obligingly, for those myopic people who did not see him so [marked by genius]. [. . .]

– Provided that the glass above did not suffer damage! Translates a worry that formerly darkened wakefulness when life questions and renews itself.

Nothing, despite the political accident that intruded into the pure glass, I know the one that concerns you, Tailhade, was harmed: protected by fragility against the violence by its pre-emptive shattering in the leading of its variegation, from which not a single inflamed piece already coloured by passion, gem, coat, smile, lily, is missing in your dazzling Rose Window, awaited for the very reason that it first of all simulates in a suspension or a defiance, the bursting forth [*éclat*], the only one, which by profession irradiates [*irradie*] the unharmed spirit of the poet.

This is an extraordinary piece of writing, not just for its poetic acrobatics and allusiveness but for its sustained meditation on poetry and destruction, literature and criminal damage. It is worth drawing out in some detail. The act of terror is senseless and nihilistic, but also full of significance. It is there to be interpreted, or, to follow the motif of brokenness and reconstitution, it needs to be 'pieced together'. We can see this in the way Mallarmé builds the essay around dichotomies: meaning/non-meaning, chaos/order, brokenness/wholeness. The references to glass are an allusion to Tailhade's book of poems, *Vitraux* (1891), and Mallarmé never hesitates to pay homage to his friends. Tailhade is the hero of the piece – he was also, in a nice irony, the only one injured. Moreover, it is likely that the bomb was made and perhaps even 'planted' (the pun exists in French too) by Félix Fénéon, a friend of both Mallarmé's and Tailhade's, another literary anarchist, and one of the greatest modern art critics of the time. One writer blowing up another writer with similar views is a rare concretisation of the literary world's self-referentiality, a kind of explosive short-circuiting of the avant-garde community. It is a sign of the theatricalised nature of the times that Tailhade had previously professed sympathy with the anarchist campaigns, and continued to do so from the hospital bed after he was injured (he admired 'the beautiful gesture').

Then there is the '*pot de fleur*'. The bomb was a terracotta flowerpot packed with nails and explosives, covered with a lid, and with a fuse sticking out (a model of the original bomb can still be seen in the museum of the Préfecture de Police in Paris). The image evoked by Mallarmé is of the fuse sticking out like some headless flower. He calls the fuse its '*tige*', its stalk, and grafts onto this deadly simulacrum of horticulture his own ideal flower. We think of Mallarmé's famous quotation from his preface to René Ghil's *Traité du Verbe* (1886): 'I say, a flower! and beyond the oblivion to which my voice consigns any contour, insofar as it is something other than the known calyx, there arises musically the idea itself, so suave, the absent one from every bouquet.'

Poetry is protected by its fragility: broken and reconfigured into a *rosace*, a rose window, its stained glass pieces are held together in beautiful patterns by the lead ribbing (*plomb*, lead, also French slang for bullets) of poetry. To be so held together, they must also be broken – poetry is what has already incorporated and survived the damage. Mallarmé's text describes cohesion, harmony, but also destruction, a smashing into pieces. And why is it a rose window? Because the rose window illuminates what lies outside for those inside – Mallarmé's images of flames, explosions (*éclater*) and irradiation connect the poem to the act of terror through powerful verbs of revelation and illumination.

Mallarmé has other things to say about bombs. In a survey on anarchism in 1893 he gave a single answer to the question of terrorism: '*Je ne sais pas d'autre bombe, qu'un livre*' – 'I know of know other bomb than a book'. Called to testify, in 1894, on behalf of Fénéon, who was on trial for possessing detonators, Mallarmé's defence was that 'There were, for Mr Fénéon, no better detonators than his articles' – hardly a denial of his friend's culpability. This constant drive towards the metaphorisation of violence, of detonators, fuses, nail-bomb-cum-flowerpots, might seem just a way of tapping into the language of violence while keeping one's hands clean of the mess. But it is more than this. There is in Mallarmé a political dimension in which literature and radical action stem from the same sources (extremism, gratuitousness, irrelevance, desperation) and share if not a language then at least a set of common images. They also, I think, share a sense of the disjointedness of the world, the brokenness of time. Far from being uninterested in politics, Mallarmé saw politics in everything, precisely because he saw artistic debate, and consideration of the role of poetry in particular, as political by its very nature.

I would even suggest that the poet who sees time itself as crisis, and the sentence as a microcosmic tessellation of crises, interruptions, intervals and resolutions, takes more than a passing or touristic interest in the world of radical politics.

Abolishing the Present

As well as radical politics, the period's 'burning issues' we could say, Mallarmé engages uniquely with what might be seen as his period's flotsam of trivia. Here too, however, the big themes of time and linearity are treated. In 1874, three years after the Commune and siege of Paris, Mallarmé single-handedly ran a fashion magazine, *La Dernière Mode* (*The Latest Fashion*). Except for poems and short prose by friends (who appear in *propriae personae*) Mallarmé wrote all of it himself, producing editorials, setting out recipes and *toilettes*, and answering readers' letters, under a variety of pseudonyms: Miss Satin, Ix, Marguerite de Ponty. The date of the magazine is important: parts of Paris still lay in ruins from the Commune and the siege three years earlier. The memory of the thousands of murdered communards, and the streets flowing with blood, was fresh enough, but Mallarmé's magazine was all about recipes, new clothes, day trips for the ladies. On the surface, *La Dernière Mode* appears to be the ultimate symbolist-decadent enterprise: pure escapism into elevated trivia, done in the spirit of intellectual cross-dressing.

Mallarmé starts the first issue's editorial (as Marguerite de Ponty) with an oddly gnomic, but also quite specific, declaration:

> Too late to speak of the summer Fashions and too soon to speak of those of winter (or even of autumn): even though several large Parisian fashion houses are already preparing, to our knowledge,

their end of season selection. Today, in fact, not having to hand the
necessary elements to begin designing a new toilette, we would like
to chat with our readers about objects which serve to complete the
toilette: Jewels. Paradox? No: is there not, in Jewels, something
perm-anent, and which befits a fashion chronicle, destined to wait to
know what fashions are in store from July to September?

The editorial seems to glory in the fact that there is nothing yet to
write about, and ends: 'our eyes dazzled by irisations, opalisations and
scintillations, might we not look at something so particularly vague
as the Future'. 'Irisations' and 'scintillations' fill Mallarmé's poems,
and there are many instances where Madame de Ponty's meditations
on clothes and accessories touch on Mallarméan themes.

What we notice first here are her flagrant capitalisations of
'Fashion' and 'Jewels', not in themselves especially remarkable, but
which come full circle, in this piece of fashion writing, in the last
word of the editorial, the 'Future'. This word, *Avenir* in French
(literally, the 'to-come'), closes off this musing on how, in a world
where the fashion writer has nothing to write about in the present,
she can at least contemplate an elusive future. In fashion terms,
declares Madame de Ponty, we have to put our final touches in first,
because the present is . . . not there. We think of her alter-ego, the
Prince of Poets, declaring: 'There is no present [. . .] the present does
not exist.'

This abolished present is the time of *La Dernière Mode*. Fashion
writing, and the business of writing a *chronique*, posits the need to
write, over and above there being anything to write about. As
Marguerite de Ponty tells us, our aspiration to what is solid and
permanent (jewels) comes not from its intrinsic value, but from the
fact that we cannot grasp what is fleeting, passing, temporary.
Madame de Ponty's article is crawling with words of temporality: it's
'too late', 'too soon'. The moment of writing is always out of step with
its subject: 'Today,' she says, is a time of empty-handedness ('*n'ayant
pas sous la main*'), and later in the passage the only reference to the
present is when she talks of a '*harmonie naturelle abolie dans le présent*',
a 'natural harmony abolished in the present'. The poet who called his
own period an 'interregnum' writes, here, in strikingly similar terms as

a fashion journalist. But the poet makes it his business to write his way out of that interregnum, to escape the messy *betweenness* of the present. The fashion writer gets stuck into it.

It is possible to see *La Dernière Mode* as the inverted image of Mallarmé's poetry – not least because the poetry itself contains so many jewels, bibelots and haunted items of interior decoration. *La Dernière Mode* is thus also the ultimate Symbolist project. The frenzy of description only draws the eye towards the consuming hollowness beneath, just as the 'chronicles' draws the reader towards the vacuum of the present. The Symbolist bric-a-brac is there (fans, lace, soft lighting, luxurious fabrics), yet for all the elegant locutions, the beautiful objects and clothes, the overall effect is dark and troubling. But Mallarmé is also concerned with consumerism and consumption – where Symbolism busily cuts off the price tags of its luxurious objects, in a sort of quest for purity and immateriality, *La Dernière Mode* replaces them, sets them back into their marketable and domestic contexts, something no Symbolist would deign to do. The link between language and subject may be sundered, but the link between the object and its price is correspondingly emphasised. *La Dernière Mode* shows Symbolism's repressed consumerism coinciding with the age's greatest anxieties.

If we dissociate Madame de Ponty's chronicle (all of her chronicles are pretty much like this) from what it purports to be talking about (clothes and jewellery), we have a rather unsettling piece. What can you not perceive *as itself*? The present moment. Where are you, always and continuously? *Between*. Certainly, that phrase 'destined to wait', were it not for the fact that what is being talked about seems flighty and frivolous, would seem a rather hopeless and dark statement about the nature of writing, as well as about the nature of time and waiting. We might be tempted to say, in a rather intellectualising way, that Mallarmé is smuggling into a piece of fashion journalism a typically unsettling set of propositions – about time and time-perception, about value, permanence and ephemerality – and to see the *Dernière Mode* editorials as 'Trojan horses' from which ideas of a different, more threatening order clamber out. We could see Madame de Ponty's chronicle as a kind of contrapuntal discourse, with lightness and whimsicality on the surface, and a more solemn, darker beat underneath. But to think that would be to miss the fact that, as Mallarmé understood, fashion discourse is the perfect means of addressing issues of temporality, prediction, value and judgement, and that it provides a language whose dilemmas and concerns are so inbuilt as to equip it uniquely to carry out such meditations.

Fashion writing emphasises the unavailability of the present, of one's own time and one's own consciousness of it; it points to the incremental catastrophe of time passing (in a Beckettian sense) that sweeps away all we do in waves of banalising trivia. Where poetry may try to repair that damage (all the while, of course, depending on it for its own necessity), fashion discourse more frankly lays bare the condition of language's fruitless striving towards subject, form's endless pursuit of content. Where poetry might try to provide the 'jewel' as consolation (and try to sell it to us as the harder-won gain), the fashion journal takes its chances with the flux.

Coupled with this way of engaging with time in *La Dernière Mode* are references to quite specific forms of attention that hinge on verbs like '*entrevoir*' (literally to 'see between', glimpse, catch sight of) and '*feuilleter*' (to flick through, leaf, browse). In fact, the forms of reading alluded to in *La Dernière Mode* are almost exclusively to do with the voluptuous flicking-through of pages that masks, through its luxury and languor, its own radical disconnectedness. We never see the thing whole or the object intact, but in traces, partially, interlopingly. Rather as in a Symbolist poem, in fact, and we might recall that the verb '*entrevoir*' and the neologism '*entrevision*' were staples of Symbolist poetic language. Indeed, the reader never actually *reads La Dernière Mode*, and the verb '*lire*' is rarely used. Instead she leafs through it, turning half-read pages in no narrative order; the eye ranges over the journal, full of interruptions and gaps, at a distance from the page and its contents, which themselves are constantly announcing their own removal from their defining subject, their own distance from the ungrippable material they are holding forth on: the present.

In Mallarmé's 'conventional' prose, the sentence is crammed with subject – time is crisis, form straining to accommodate its content. In his fashion journalism, it is the other way around, as the prose chases its elusive subject across the expensively illustrated pages of *La Dernière Mode*. Writing here is form empty of content – time is imagined as a vacuum. Mallarmé is a poet of absence, and nowhere is that absence better achieved than in fashion journalism, for the very reason that fashion journalism is never still: it is a species of absence that is dynamic and unresting, writing that is at once exultantly nonchalant and tragically alienated. Fashion writing is what poetry would be if poetry conquered its desire to outlast and outvalue its subject. *La Dernière Mode* seems, like all so-called 'marginalia' such as his '*poésie de circonstance*' (written on fans and chocolate boxes), his notes for *Anatole's Tomb* or his 'occasional' prose pieces, essential to his oeuvre. There is no 'marginal Mallarmé' any more.

It's in his prose writings that we see Mallarmé's engagement with both time and his times. What makes them so extraordinary – beyond their grace, humour and intellectual athleticism – is the way in which they reveal a poet who early on realised that any fool could make something permanent, any half-decent writer could produce a work of art that would transcend the present of its making. The trick was to inhabit time, not to escape it, to find a way of writing that did not simply look for the next exit but that could, *in its form* as distinct from just its topical content, grapple with the very conditions in which we experience time and *our times*, and how the two unfold, overlap and bifurcate.

The Age of the Empty Chair

In Monet's *The Beach at Trouville*, it is week one of the Franco-
    Prussian war.
The chair lodges in the sand between two women. One reads,
    the other

points her face at the emptying beach. The chair belongs to
    no one,
it is a found chair, a *trouvaille*, and there is never one chair
    too many

but one sitter too few. A flag rigid on its pole indicates
a swelling in the air, or something stronger, and the rent waves,

delicate turmoils of spume and lace, are distant cousins of the
    revolution
bound into the ebb and flow it breaks free of, then breaks back
    into.

There is sand in the paint; the place is mixed into its making
and even the brushstrokes replicate the water's peaks as they take

the light: rooves pell-mell across a city skyline, flashpoints in
    the sun.
The chair suggests all that can be suggested about change, but
    it remains

apart from it: the way a sail suggests the wind, the way a shell holds
a recording of the waves even as the waves turn around it.

Six Poems

SEÁN LYSAGHT

The Burning City

Wader Sweeney
wanted to get to the burning city
but the river was wide at that point   he lost time

crossing over   taking both shores   downwind
he could smell the burning   he flew again
with a flock of undecided dunlins

they switched directions over the dark water   he said
'No it's this way'   his words a redshank
scolding the others   he could smell the burning city

the main emotions   on the stiffening wind
pushing the wildfowl back he laboured on
upstream   'What about the kids
in the pleading city?'   his words a curlew

bubbling under the ideal note
when a farmer dropped a crowbar on a stone
the birds detonated in every direction

Sweeney wanted to shout 'It's upstream
to the smouldering city!' 'This way'
said the ringed plover's plaintive note

in all the confusion as the smell changed
and the first soldier kicked over the rubble
of the ruined city

A Tubenose Skull

As they combed the beaches for Sweeney
they came across an empty shell,

a tubenose skull at the end of earth,
its hooked mandible

still remembering the bending sea.
They whispered 'fulmar'

to this rare pelagic flower;
but their lore was no match

for the saga of the ledges,
when a walnut brain

and a fringe of feathers
could contain those calling cliffs.

So the plated beak
became a mask to fit on manners,

a double-barrel breath
steeling the will

to the first drop over an ocean
where Sweeney fell

and then carried on
in the briny stations,

winging it
through every distraction of the weather.

In the Wilderness

Sweeney whistled in the mouth of a river;
he was wigeon.

He dived in the surf of a lake;
he was smew.

His call came through from the stars,
as the wind reared on the guyrope of midnight;
he was redwing.

He tickled the toes of the reeds in their beds;
he was dabchick.

He fenced on a catwalk of glittering water;
he was grebe.

He fell from the dome of the day
to the floor of the earth;
he was falcon.

Then he was phalarope, flitting in the hills of the grey sea.

Or shearwater, just clear of the waves in the wings of his life.

Eventually, he tilted homeward.

But the cleric had spotted him.

All of a sudden
he roared out 'Sweeney!'

And that spoiled everything.

Heron Sweeney

Heron Sweeney rattled
the long stilts of his undercarriage.
These must be for water, he thought,
as he flew to a lake margin.

There he stalked his own reflection,
step by step,
his impossible neck
and the yellow eyes
with their alloy of hunger.

The raised cone of his bill
scattered the fish shadows.
He thought, 'How can I smile?
How can I socialise,
with a dagger for laughter?'

The water was a better mirror
than the tinsel and glare
he'd gathered as a man
to meet only an anxious face
or his own stretched features
on the bend of a spoon.

Sweeney studied the heron so slowly,
he looked like a reed –
and grabbed an eel,
a new, elaborate moustache
dripping back to the mirror.

He shook his head;
it didn't suit.

By then it was evening;
he shrieked to the dusk
and lifted his frame
clear of the reeds and willows.

Sweeney Exposed

He knew too much.
He could mimic Emberizidae.
He flew with Laridae over spring fields.
He played 'Hands up!' with a parliament of shags.
He conformed to a squadron of snipe
banking down over a drumlin in the evening.

His naked rage still troubled him,
but he got on so well with the generae
he couldn't expose the tree
where he knew a squatting yahoo
was defiling placid horses.

He loved every adopted form,
dabbling and diving,
swinging a long sifting bill in shallows,
teasing a little flatfish
through a May afternoon –
it was all so interesting!
Everything became him.

And still, his conscience kept painting
a pre-lapsarian man
with a hanging scrotum,
a screeching bonobo monkey,
to show all his successes were forgeries.

Sweeney's Quills

As Sweeney moulted
his wings delivered quills.

The first of these produced handbills announcing a play.
Others composed sonnets to murderers and sea-captains.
They signed their names to the deaths of loyal subjects,
penned satires, squibs, and broadsides
mocking the mob, or mocking the mob's king.
For this, one had his tongue nailed to a gatepost,
another poisoned himself on the dreams
that would leak from his quill,
till another again trimmed it, and took the feather on,
still claiming a whole world's rule
for the dance of his ink,
that this was the only dance in town, or out.
But no one noticed. They were all too busy crafting
steel for a nib.
Quills were passé.
So the old masters
stayed in their towers to pore over
the flight of a glorious feather, in another time,
and played the games that only
they could play: esoteric, remote,
but possessed of such strength
they made a quill-master famous.

Even in the computer age,
some feathers trimmed,
and sleeved in ink,
could startle a virgin page.

Sweeney flew on, in the throes of a moult.
He stopped on a wire
strung across an empty moor
to pull more flakes from his breast.
These would line a pipit's nest,
they used to say,
but they just blew away
with spindrift into nothing.

To Sweeney's relief.

Six Sonnets

GIUSEPPE GIOACHINO BELLI
1791–1863

Translated with an introduction by Peter N. Dale

Giuseppe Gioachino Belli is perhaps the most prolific, innovative and imaginative sonneteer on record, and yet mention of his name registers but a faint quaver on the critical seismograph of literary awareness. In Italy, certainly, his reputation is secure. Abroad however, while rare critics, Harold Bloom among them, readily recognise his canonical stature, general critical taste seldom takes his measure.

Difficulties in translating his oeuvre account in good part for the relative neglect. True, Eleanor Clark's initial skirmish with the serried ranks of his poetry brought back reports of the power of his densely marshalled sonnetry, and stimulated further forays by Harold Norse, Miller Williams, Robert Garioch, William Neill, Allen Andrews and several others. But the effect of their versions, most of which reworked a handful of the more famous sonnets, was minor.[1] Anthony Burgess stands out as an exception. A deep admirer of the Roman poet, he would have undertaken, had he had life enough and time, a complete rendition of the corpus into English. Faced however with the immensity of the task, he limited his intervention to a short elegant novel on the poet, and his fictional alter ego's struggle with, and failure before, the sheer rockface of giddily steep translation.

This fate of foreign neglect or silence becomes comprehensible when we consider what Belli undertook to do. In little more than two decades, he penned over two thousand sonnets (2279 to be exact), which constitute a prismatic series of remarkably vivid snapshots of the inner world of Romans and of their lives during the period from 1828 to 1849. Yet it is not the sheer volume which intimidates a foreign readership, even if its exuberantly insistent rhythmic evocations of everyday life under the Popes can prove exacting of the strongest readers. Belli was a hyperrealist (albeit one wedded to the surrealistic substrates of our language-driven imaginings) who, to render that intensely provincial backwater authentically, made it speak to us through the precisely captured cadences of the speech of its illiterate lumpen proletariat. *Bref*, he composed his magisterial opera in pure dialect, one rendered with a precisian's ear for punctilious phonetic redress. Yet it is exactly this uncompromising fidelity to transcriptional rectitude in recording a hirsute demotic that makes his verse somewhat recalcitrant to the probing gaze and pricklish ear of the rank outsider.

Stifled by what he felt to be the etiolated airs of an exhausted and exhaustively recycled literary Italian, whose atmosphere of refined conceit and tireless allusiveness had turned the vigorous workmanly brawn of the trecento's *rime* into a cadaveric *danse macabre* of effete gamesmanship, Belli threw himself into the slangy underworld of Roman street-talk, and devised his system of orthography to capture its rambunctious palaver. The artificial discourse which had otherwise allowed men of taste and learning across the manifold of distinct provinces to maintain a common identity, a *lingua franca* among literati otherwise caught up in the rich weft of local dialects, was in crisis. The heritage forged by Dante's magnificent amalgam of early vernaculars had lost contact with the fructifying ground of daily experience, and Belli, in contradistinction to Leopardi and Manzoni who both strove to 'purify the language of the tribe(s)' towards an idiom acceptable to the emerging world of a national society, plunged his creative roots down into the landscape of the most backward province of all, into the gutters of the papaline city of Rome.

Here he found another *Inferno*, devoid of all prospects of purgative redemption and paradisal recompense, the punishing mundane world of poverty, marginal life, trickster knacks and ruses for surviving on the smell of an oil-rag in a vast ramshackle society run through with religious hypocrisy and theo-bureaucratic unctuousness. The language itself was 'devilish' in its perverse genius for baroque distortions and surreal meditations, an anti-language that voiced everything that literature hitherto had censored as beneath the dignity of letters. Yet Belli's immersion in this tribal dialect and its lore allowed him to anticipate by a century much of modern anthropological technique by fully registering a pre-industrial caste of mind. In terms of literary history, the infernal panorama he contrived enabled Belli to capture, in anticipation of modernists like Joyce, the fretful effluvia of everyday consciousness.

His exacting sonnetry is quixotic in the way its flawless rhythm rides with effortless panache on the hacks and jades of the banal, the trivia of ephemeral chat, but it is for all that a chattering culture that resonates with two thousand years of experience attuned to the duress of authority's peremptory (il-)logic. In adopting this strategy he was aware that his genius would dedicate twenty years of toil to erecting a monument (the echo is Horatian) to the people of Rome who were all but silenced by its official history, and that this selfsame monument risked being time's carrion; for it was written within a sumptuously profligate lexicon, knowledge of which was fast falling into desuetude, and, these days, if not illegible to Romans themselves, then certainly demanding a slow parsing.

It has, nonetheless, at least within Italian culture, worn well, in part because standard Italian writing comfortably exploits the many varieties of regional inflection: tolerance for patois survives because so many Italians speak dialect in their homes, and great writers like Eugenio Montale, Carlo Emilio Gadda and Pier Paolo Pasolini have accommodated their native idiom to the Italian they write, or have written directly in pure dialect. The amount of scholarly attention of the first water dedicated to editing Belli's massive oeuvre, generation after generation, ranks with what we expect of editions of classical texts from antiquity. Many of his poems reside in popular memory intact verbatim, or survive as proverbial tags culled from many memorable lines, for their pungent relevance to the chronic corruptions of an aged country.

However, national literatures generally show far less tolerance for patois as a vehicle for significant meaning, poetry in particular. It is a prejudice that ignores the fact that one district's speech sounds like baloney over the border. It has been well said by Max Weinreich that a language is a dialect with a fleet to back it up. Authors like Belli sing among the disarmed, indeed, compose in the face of victorious armies of governed speech keen to conscript the rowdy, barbaric hordes on the margins into the uniformed divisions of an homogeneous modernity. In translating dialect poetry written to shout dissonantly in the face of the winner's domesticating idiom, there seems no alternative than that of choosing a comparable dialect which shares a similar regard of hispid tension with, and rebellious defiance of, an overbearing foreign mother-in-law's tongue.

A fine opportunity to set a technical example for others was lost when one of his earliest translators, Albert Zacher, abandoned his intuition that the only workable versions must be those which recast Belli's *Romanesco* into a comparable brogue. The Cologne dialect had seemed adequate, but Zacher feared for its readability in the broader German world, and hence resigned himself to literary German in translating 242 sonnets (roughly 11 per cent) for his book *Narrenspiegel der Ewigen Stadt* (1906). Robert Garioch pioneered 120 versions in Scots, and William Neill has done 17 in the same idiom. Their works are difficult to obtain, and few read Scots with ease. Most translators opt for a flat paraphrase in a standardised tongue, with an occasional vernacular gesture, in order to reach a wider audience.

There is nothing flat in Anthony Burgess's translations. His linguistic brio and formal craftsmanship give you an idea of Belli's wit. A trace of Lancashire idiom informs his versions, but they are, essentially, free rewritings in Burgess's mode[2], unshackled of strong lien and purchase on the originals which inspired them. In part, this was consequential on his decision to employ the abba abba rhyme-scheme for Belli's Petrarchan architecture. The parsimony of rhyme-words in English obliges the faithful to transgress, paying lip-service to the metaphoric play and word-sense of the seminal text in order to concentrate on preserving its music.

In translating the 2279 sonnets of the Bellian corpus, I have employed the Australian idiom I heard spoken by three generations of neighbours, friends and family as a child and boy raised on the outskirts of Melbourne, within a stone's throw of the rowdy ambience of the family hotel. Analysing, in retrospect, my own natural

reproduction of it, my scruples can detect at times a middle-class
assimilation here and there of aspects of its syntax and pronunciation
to the corrective norms of standard English. One can pick out
something of this slight, ostensibly falsifying note by comparing
these renditions with the inimitable precision of authentic street
cant in that great epic of Australian verse, C.J. Dennis's *The
Sentimental Bloke*.[3] But it is also true that the dialect had many levels,
of class, region and gender, and each underwent historical change
over the three or four decades which separate Dennis's Ginger Micks,
Doreens and Digger Smiths from the people I listened to, who had
grown up under the normative influences of national radio, the
'talkies', and later, television.

Belli's demotic, itself a dying language idiomatically
superannuated by the time he wrote it down in his maturity (hence
his many glosses), is that of an illiterate *ignobile vulgus* of scroungers,
bumpkins, bots, whores, slatterns, crims, greasers, mugs, whingers,
galahs, louts, lairs, larrikens, wowsers, shysters, shills, toffs, dags,
gossips, ne'er-do-well's and down-and-outs, a babbling Bakhtinian
carnival of marginal types hacking out a life of sorts in the cramped
slums of pre-*Risorgimento* Rome, under that Khomeiniesque *ante
litteram* theocratic state which the Roman papacy had sought to
shore up against the Reformation and, later, both the Enlightenment
and the French Revolution's rippling historical currents. Handling
this level of discourse in the rough cut and thrust of lower class
repartee typical of the old Australian underclass presents relatively
few problems. Difficulties ensue when one is forced to deal with the
transposition of a dialect instinct with the agricultural, historical and
ecclesiastical jargon of an ancient Mediterranean culture into the
pastoral, mainly urban vocabulary of a young society, pagan in
outlook and shorn of cultural depth and strong historical memory.

The advantage of this choice of idiom overall is that 90 per cent
of the translated text is relatively accessible, with a minor effort at
familiarisation, to English speakers. Many tensions remain
unresolved, and the solutions I have adopted smack of the provisory
on occasion. The rhythm of speech, for example, is that of a balladic
vernacular which may jar on ears trained to the music of the
traditional English sonnet. Aiming at a close, yet minimally rhymed

parsing as an aid for those perplexed by Belli's dialect, I have chosen to fetter the spontaneous anarchy of my dialect to the terse semantic exigencies of the original. The point of the exercise is not the hybristic one of trying to imitate or recreate Belli's genius, but simply to provide a rough map through the bristling terrain of his oeuvre. The intention has been to wedge a jemmy into that closed linguistic universe, and prise out, by cribbing linguistic leverage, the gist and flow of his Pandora's box of 'devilish' discourse. I have striven, particularly, to open it up to that rare band of foreign poets and students whose curiosity about Belli's astonishing opera is all too often defeated by the eyestrain of reading off his teasingly familiar, yet disconcertingly estranged, vernacular.[4]

This dialect of my childhood may possibly, in its own fossilised form, and in the system of transcription I have used, deflect interest.[5] In following Belli's principles I have had to compromise in one significant direction. Unlike Italian and its dialects, English and its vernaculars prove ambiguous and often unintelligible in strict phonetic transcription. I have therefore found myself constrained to compromise with regard to orthography, in order to secure a minimal level of comprehension at sight. I have, for example, retained initial 'h', though it is often ignored. Spelling has not been regularised, in order to heighten recognisability. A little familiarity with this somewhat makeshift system should enable eventual readers, via notes supplied to the originals and their Australian versions, to exploit the crib to parse the Roman text. Like Wittgenstein's ladder, my versions can be cast aside as soon as their job, that of allowing the adventurer to scale the verbal stepping-stones of the original, and work independently with it, has been done. The following six poems are samples of the technique employed.[6]

NOTES

1   After a century of desultory skirmishes, English versions of just over two hundred pieces, roughly one tenth of the corpus, exist. Up to 1983 some 640 sonnets had, by one calculation, been rendered into various foreign languages. See R. Vighi's appendix to D. Abeni, R. Bertazzoli, C.G. De Michelis, P. Ghibellini, *Belli oltre Frontiera*, Bonacci Editore, Roma, 1983, p. 373

2   Burgess himself stated in his autobiography, *You've Had Your Time* (Penguin, 1990), p. 242, that his versions were 'over-free'.

3   Dennis certainly shared Belli's compositional fluency: he wrote some four thousand poems over a similar stretch of time. Neither of course come anywhere near the rutilant flamboyance attributed to Saikaku Ihara at his improvising best, but then again, they wrote in technically more complex verse-forms.

4   J.J. Wilson was 'at once both horrified and fascinated by the strange appearance of Belli's language': A. Burgess, *ABBA ABBA* (Gorgi Books, 1977), p. 104.

5   'I sometimes thought of dedicating my life to their translation. It would have been a useless venture, for who in the Anglophone world would care about an obscure dialect poet?' Burgess, *You've had Your Time*, p. 327

6   Three of my versions have previously been published by Peter Toohey, professor of classics at Calgary University, in his *Melancholy, Love, and Time* (University of Michigan Press, 2004), pp. 316, 323, 325–6. Dr Toohey was raised within earshot of the same dialect I learnt, and generously undertook to check much of my work against his own intimate feel for its grammar and idiom.

805

The f'lofficer a the coffee-bar

The men a this wirld, well, the lod are all like
Beans in a coffee grinder as they're getten grondèd:
Wun afta r' anutha pops up as they riggle in that tite
Space, bud in the end, they're all fadèd ta be pounded.

Offen they switch pozzies, an wun'ull elbow away,
If he's bigger, the smaller bean ta the ouder.
They tumble ad each utha's heels in the doorway
Ta that meddle'ud'ull chirn'em in'a mere powder.

An that's how men live here on earth, I've foun':
Fate wirks the lodduv'em in'u'a fine blend
As it spins'em, wun an all, round an roun',

An as each wun moves, slow or strong, fat or thin,
They always sift thru, clueless, ta the boddem, an end
Up fallen down its craw as deth drinks 'em in.

1501

In vino verities

Cop this fresh off the grapevine. The curate ut came
Ta the refreshment do afta the baptism t'day
Afta'r eleven glasses god anuther, an when he'd drained
It, his brain boiled over an flipped n' this's wod he had ta say.

'Ah fuckit! Just cos he's born in the Latin rite,
Why is id a priest's allowed ta screw roun' with a whore,
But can' go an take a wife! The same thing ut's allrite,
That's a virtue, f'ra Greek's a sin fa me. It's godda be flawed!'

An then he wen' on: 'Who'll explain the why'n wherefore
A this puzzle a mine? Who c'n loosen the knot?
Nod even St Joseph cud, even if he used his saw.

Wot's a root got ta do with the way ya speak?
Wot's the big diff b'tween, say, a wife that's got
A latin cunt an anuther with a twat that's greek?'

535

The wimen a Rome

There's no village anywhere'ut's got wimen that c'n
Stan' c'mparison with the wimen here in Rome
The way they treat c'nfessionals like a secund home,
So each c'n call'aself a good upstanden chrischun.

Acorse ev'ry last wunnuv'em'ull have a trace a the pro,
An they'll suck their husbens dry spenden their wages;
But when it cums ta be'en devout, cripes, they go
Off ta church at the drop uva hat. Been like that f'r ages.

Wodda they give the wirld? Only their foul flesh, mate,
N' that's just a filthy bag a wurms. But their harts
Go out ta the Church, they do: I'll tell ya that strait.

An when it cums ta the Sacred House uv our Lord,
They got such a pashenut frenzy f'rit, ut the tarts
Go flirten there, an in church, uv offen scored.

67

The mem'ry

When they strung up Gammardella, the day he carked it
Was the same wun I was cunfirmed on, as I recall.
I got a donut cake n' a toy made uva string an a ball
That me godfather bort me f'ra prezzie at the market.

An then me dad wen'n fetched a coach fa the day,
But first he wannèd t'enjoy the site a the bloke they hung.
So he hauled me up on'a'ris sholders, n' sed as he swung
Me up: 'Cop that gibbet! Ain't she a bewdy, ay!'

An just as Johnno the hangman finished off the job
Wiff a swift kick up the coit t'wiz client, me dad
Lashed out n' ga' me a backanda fair in me gob.

'Take that,' he sed, 'an jus' rememba, too,
The same fate's ritten in the stars fa, lad,
A fousen uvvers ut are much much bedder'n yu.'

85

Keep yer 'an's ta yaself,
n' ya mowf in yer own shit

Ouch! Bugg'rit! Don' pinch me, ya prick!
Wodya reckun, ut me bum's as soft as straw?
It's fleshy; an I ain't got woollies on, an wot's more,
This slip a taffetta thad I'm wearen ain't thick.

Chat me up as ya like, call me a swine, f'rinstance,
Say I'm a pro . . . a bug . . . , but keep ya mitts off me.
'Paw games are poor louts' games', ya see,
N yors are like a flamen pair a pincers.

Stop it, I tell ya, ya ruddy yeller-faced mutt.
Lay off'a me: an if ya like it soft n' pappy,
Then have a go at maulen Trudie's butt.

I gotcha marked down, Phil. I've crossed yer out.
Off now are ya? Ah just the ticket ta make me happy.
Praised be the Lord! Ya pencilneck, ya lout.

185

New Wine

When Noah saw his vinyèd bursten with plenny
(An it was under his mansion's walls, rite next t'wis home)
An how on wunna the burgeonen vines, a bunch'd grown
That musta weighed ten poun', or p'raps even twennie,

He squeezed the sauce from them grapes in'a'ris mowf
N' sed: 'Bonzer! Fuck! Wodda bluddy bonzer drop!'
But not be'en used ta hangovers, he wen' over the top,
Tasted far too much, an ended up hurten himself.

Ta cut fings short, that juice there played the sorda trick
It duz nowadays on the rest uv us, as any pisspot can tell,
When we're stonkered so bad, we tumble down arse over tit.

An since he di'n' nav any dacks on when he fell,
As wunna them verses has in the Holy Rit,
'He showed'em his roger n' knackers as well.'

Two Poems

DEREK MAHON

Chorus from *Antigone*

after Sophocles

Wonders are many and none
more wonderful than man
whose sail and plunging prow
cleave a windswept path
through life-threatening seas;
who opens the rich earth
year after year with his
worn-out, unwavering plough.

Our visionary technology
outwits the throbbing thrush,
creatures of land and sea,
the bear and the octopus,
and tames the ravening beast
in thicket and upland gorse.
A lion bites the dust;
we bridle the wild horse.

The Yellow Nib, Vol. 2, 2006, pp. 99–101

Our wide-ranging resources,
so beneficial, can also
serve evil purposes.
We honour those who show
due reverence to the divine
but spurn the sinful man;
blinded by his own pride,
he walks a lonely road.

With speech and intuitions
born in the lightning brain
we create civilizations,
shelter from wind and rain.
Each difficult circumstance,
crisis, disease or pain,
inspires us; only against
death do we strive in vain.

Ariel to Prospero

after Rilke

Deposed magician, tricked of your worldly throne,
you kept this spirit to keep an eye on you,
knowing in due course you would let me go;
but, strict in daylight, ruminative at night,
you made up reasons to postpone my flight.
My servitude, as you know, implies your own –
think of the music if our bonds were gone,
a new earth music previously unknown
even in this noisy island; think how brave
to waive your art, vacate your vatic cave
and live in the real world, breathing the air
blown to us daily in our exile here.
I flit and whistle at your slightest whim,
bored but amused by this strange interim,
and smile to think of the odd things I know:
mysterious defiles where wildflowers grow,
the secret places where new species thrive;
I've a light work-load, scope for initiative . . .
Be frank, will you shed a tear when it is time?

('The cloud-capp'd towers, the gorgeous palaces'
leave not a rack behind; we hide our faces
and listen patiently as the restored duke,
doubtful about the future, drowns his book
with a few lines noted for calm restraint,
reliant on his own strength 'which is most faint'.)

Six Poems

GARY ALLEN

Easter

The open mouths of the ornamental fish heads
are dried dust

wives tie printed headscarves
firmly under their chins –

where are you father?
you are early this year

as the cold deceptive sun.

Your yellow skin a fine film
stretched tight as on a drum
around the bare trees

your tea-stained face
the children roll down the green hills

as they look for you in the sandpits
down avenues
under the looped wire of the disused tennis courts.

Listen to the lovers
rising through the ground

hands stroking thighs
easy as ducks on the dam

soft as snow falling on the flower beds.

And above everything she sits
dry-eyed statue of the Sciences

bigger than the park
the whooping children

more faithful than empty cupboards
bridal gowns, backstreet bookies

or all the mournful chapel bells.

The Mechanic

And it rained all day again
the fields and lanes
thick with the muck of it

a false light towards evening
shimmering high above the Cross:

you smell everything rotting

the potatoes in the heavy soil
the accumulated layers of the bogland –

memories we try to hold.

The rusted parts of this motorbike
lying in the yard

should have been buried with you
as you cower this sodden night
in Crebilly's overcrowded churchyard,

like a well-oiled rifle barrel.

This is the sum of us
nothing less or more

as I come down the firebreak
in a futile trick
that I am risking something

the sound of rain in the dark pines
that are never dense enough

the dog already lost
and keeping to my heels.

Lord, you have suffered for our sins
but we have suffered too

not knowing what it is to be blessed
among the ordinary,
or to die in salutation.

The Sea

Thirty steps lead up to old rooms
of infested wood and hardboard partitions, leaking taps –

and Jesus said, Let those who have sinned
let them dwell in darkness:

my love scrubs the dry skin from her hair
under cold water

her heavy bare breasts pressed against the washing-board

for the English man who will take her between carriages
who will sleep in our bed with his happy children.

I see your mother lying on the sofa
her sixties skirt pulled high above her thighs

and the men who pass through the rooms ignore her –

your father with his tiny Luftwaffe planes
his aerodynamic books, handful of receipts

his colleague in deceit and new-built classrooms,
the Iranian below who brings his wife to watch –

and Jesus sits with the girls in the shunting yards
asking us why we prostitute ourselves for flesh:

are you aware of the sea, my love?
it is everywhere beyond the polders

one day it will wash over the thresholds of all our rooms –

your mother's heart will swell and burst with the salt of it
you will suffocate by the bottleful
your father play with coloured building blocks

and I will not escape by crossing shores
or fooling Jesus with a different mindset to the dead
as I hover in the white space you once called poems.

The Gallows

Light snow eddies
like white water round the streetlight,

round my feet –

I am between two houses
the one I left where the librarian sleeps
smug before the imitation fire

the dimmed lamps
where we read my poems, that are now hers

and the one I was going to
before I stopped below this hill
where traitors were hanged and left to dangle

devoured by birds who took the dead hair
to line their nests.

The second house is hard water
smells of iron and oil
work boots standing ready on the table
where no one has their own bed –

here dreams are pecked to death.

Oceanography

Sometimes a thought will suggest itself:
it is mid-winter, the island ferry is disabled in the harbour
its rusted chain sagging with bladder wrack
the tailgate clanging with the swell.

These rocks are hard and unforgiving
Dissenters' faith, family laws
promises easily given –

great mountains that once roared
and moved to cool in these waves.

Where does the sea take them?
small boats fragile as matchwood
out to Faeroese or Icelandic waters

and brings them back again
down deep channels, secret currents,
spewed up all along this shore

swollen bodies, fish-eaten faces,
once they were claimed
by the knitting pattern on their jerseys

up here on Torneady Point
girls would sometimes wait up to a year –

imagine, that cold eye fixed upon this expanse
vast and empty as the thoughts in your mind, my love
those little origami napkins
dropped from the end deck of the outgoing ferry.

My thoughts are clear as January
sharp as the wind that howls
through the caverns of the ruined castle –

henna hair, looped earrings, birthmarks,
big as the ocean chart
quiet as a prayer, a morning walk along this pebbled beach.

Fusion

This house sleeps in the sun
a quiet afternoon
the yellow curtain fluttering at the door –

listen Lord for I am alone
as if the mind has become the universe:

I am eight years old and hear everything

the milk curdling in their saucepans of water
the dog panting under the kitchen table

the sigh of clothes dropping to the floor
in the little shady room above.

Jesus is my family
looking down from the wall
judging a greater sin than is mine

forty years in a distant future.

And the breadman is in the street –
the great wooden box of a radio
talks of stars burning out

as everything meets to a centre –

my hand full of coin
the bitter leaves on the lime trees
his face stilled above hers

the deafening roar of gelignite
outside the garage – then dust.

'Whose Woods These Are . . .'
Some Aspects of Poetry and Translation

CIARAN CARSON

*A version of an inaugural lecture given as Professor of Poetry
at Queen's University Belfast, 5 May 2005*

Whose woods these are I think I know.
His house is in the village though;
He will not see me stopping here
To watch his woods fill up with snow.

My little horse must think it queer
To stop without a farmhouse near
Between the woods and frozen lake
The darkest evening of the year.

He gives his harness bells a shake
To ask if there is some mistake.
The only other sound's the sweep
Of easy wind and downy flake.

The woods are lovely, dark and deep.
But I have promises to keep,
And miles to go before I sleep,
And miles to go before I sleep.

The Yellow Nib, Vol. 2, 2006, pp. 112–127
© Ciaran Carson
'Stopping by Woods on a Snowy Evening' © Robert Frost

I cannot remember what day it was when I gave a reading in the University of Massachusetts at Amherst, the erstwhile home of Robert Frost. I cannot even remember the year. It was some time ago. But I do remember that before I read my own poems, I recited the poem quoted above, 'Stopping by Woods on a Snowy Evening'. Earlier on that day I had gone to Robert Frost's house, although, when I came to the door, I found it locked. I thought of lines from another Amherst poet, Emily Dickinson: 'The soul selects her own society / Then shuts the door . . .' At any rate, I felt obliged to pay the spirit of Robert Frost some homage. And reading his poem afforded me a way into my own poems. At the end of the reading, an old, snowy-haired man dressed in an oatmeal tweed suit came up to me and said: 'Mr Carson, the last time I heard "Stopping by Woods on a Snowy Evening" being recited aloud, it was by Robert Frost, and he was standing where you are standing now.' A shiver went down my spine. I felt the shade of Robert Frost. As if I'd had a little hallucination, not knowing who was who. And for an instant I was lost again in the snowy landscape of his poem. I felt betwixt and between. I am reminded, now, of some lines from another poem of Frost's, 'The Hill Wife': 'I wonder how far down the road he's got / He's watching from the woods, as like as not.'

The next day I was brought to read at the John Boyle O'Reilly Club at Springfield, Massachusetts. I confess that until then I had not heard of the name of John Boyle O'Reilly. I have since learned that he was born in County Meath in 1844, and that at the age of nineteen, after joining the Fenian Society, he enlisted in the 10th Hussars with the object of spreading disaffection among the Irish soldiers. He was found out, tried for high treason, and sentenced to be shot. The sentence was commuted to life imprisonment: he was sent to Dartmoor, and then to the penal colony of Bunbury, near Fremantle in Australia. In 1869 he escaped in an open boat and was picked up by the American ship *Gazelle*. To cut a long story short, he spent the rest of his life in America, where he became a prominent speaker for the Irish cause, and a novelist and poet of some reputation. Many of his works deal with the condition of exile. He died in 1890 from an overdose of chloral hydrate. Suicide was suspected, but could not be proven.

My hosts took me down the Massachusetts Turnpike to a Howard Johnson's motel. It transpired that the John Boyle O'Reilly Club was located underneath the motel, and was accessed by a door you wouldn't have known was there had you not known it was there. I went down a steep flight of stairs and found myself in another world – for all the world like an Irish bar, with a horseshoe mahogany counter and wooden booths. An old lady dressed in green came up to me with a heavy tome of a book in her hands, and asked if I might recite from it before I read my own poems. The book had a green tooled binding and was entitled *John Boyle O'Reilly: His Life, Poems and Speeches.* I could hardly say no. I read from the book. I will come back to what I read in due course.

I read my poems. I played the flute, and sang a song in Irish. When I had finished, I went to the bar, where I was introduced to a group of four men in their seventies or eighties, and their wives. They had been talking in American English, and I took them for Americans, until one man addressed me in clear Munster Irish:

> 'Carb as tú, a dhuine uasail?' – 'Where are you from, sir?'
> 'As Béal Feirste mé,' I replied. – 'I am from Belfast.'
> 'Béal Feirste in Éirinn?' – 'Belfast, Ireland?'

I replied in the affirmative. There was a little collective murmur of astonishment that someone from Belfast, Ireland, could speak Irish. It turned out that these four men were among the few surviving natives of Inishvickillane, one of the Blasket Islands, from whence the population had emigrated en masse to Springfield, Massachusetts, some fifty years previously. They had arrived in America with little English. They learned American English. They married American girls. 'It's lovely when they get to talk that Gaelic with someone,' said one of the wives.

We got to talking some more, and to singing. One man sang me a version of 'An Sceilpín Draighneach', 'The Lone Thorn Tree'. Here's the first verse:

> Agus maidin chiúin dar éiríos
> is amach faoi bhruach na gcoillte

Ansin sea buaileadh an saighead liom
is mo leigheas ni raibh le fáil
Nó gur dhearc mé an bhruinneal mheidheartha
faoi bhruach an sceilpe draighneach
Agus gheit mo chroí le meidhir aici
is dheamhan éirigh liom í fháil

A quiet morning as I arose
From under the shelter of the woods
'Twas there the arrow pierced me through
With no cure to be found
For I beheld the comely maid
Under the shade of the lone thorn tree
And my heart thrilled to see her there
Though she would ne'er be mine.

We know that thorn trees are associated with the fairy world; so whether the encounter is with a woman of this world or that is open to question. The song is a type of *aisling*,[1] in which, typically, the author of the song falls asleep in a wood or by a hedge, and has a dream of a beautiful fairy woman who is an embodiment of the spirit of Ireland. She calls on him to help free Ireland from foreign domination. And this song, 'An Sceilpín Draighneach', is also a song of exile from that dream world. The last verse goes:

Agus rachfaidh mé má fhéadaim
Go Meiriceá i dtús an tséasúir
San áit nach mbeidh mo ghaolta
Ar an taobh ná tíocht romham
Is ni fhillfhidh mé ar m'ais go hÉirinn
Ná go labharfaidh an cuach san ngeimhreadh
Is caisleán ag mo mhuintir
Sé bheith tóigthe ar bhruach an chuain.

And I will go as well I might
To America come next season
Where those related to me

Are nowhere to be seen
And I will not return to Ireland
Till the cuckoo speaks in winter
And my people have a castle
Built on the harbour side.

The Inishvickillane men that I met never returned to Ireland. No cuckoo sang in winter. No impossible castle was built on the harbour side. I've translated *bruach an chuain* as 'harbour side'. *Bruach* is a bank, a boundary, an edge, and I'm interested in that edge as an interregnum between two worlds: a border that is concerned with that which is, and that which is not. I think of the dreamy alternatives posed in 'Stopping by Woods on a Snowy Evening', and the vast speculative gap that opens up between

And miles to go before I sleep

and

And miles to go before I sleep.

The double take of those lines makes us read the poem again in their light, for the second 'And miles to go before I sleep' is a comment on the first, an adumbration, an alternative reading; it is a kind of translation.

I think about two languages. Back in the 1950s – in the last millennium – I'd lie awake in bed at night saying words over to myself. I would have been three going on four, or four going on five, on the cusp of two languages. Unusually for Belfast at the time, our family spoke Irish at home. English was banned, so I must have picked it up from the street. As dusk came on I would lie awake listening to the sounds of the street: children who were allowed to stay up later than me, skipping, running, chanting, playing hide-and-seek or war games. Sometimes I'd hear a horse pass by, drawing a rumbling empty coal-cart or a brewer's dray, and I would say the word *horse* over to myself, savouring its strangeness. It sounded nothing like the Irish *capall*: it was, indeed, a horse of another colour, a matter ponderably different to the onomatopoetic Latinate kick of *capall*. As the horse's hooves clopped and faded into the distance, I'd hear a ghostly echo of the English *cobble*, the obdurate fist-sized stones with which some of the streets were still paved, and which would be used as ammunition for the riots of the 1960s and 70s. *Horse, capall, cobble, horse, capall, cobble, horse* . . . I'd say the words over and over to myself, rounding the syllables in my mouth until the meanings would wear out of them, and they'd drop like nonsense pebbles into the dark well of sleep.

Later in life I'd come to ponder the significance of my own name, itself a kind of nonsense, a contradiction, an oxymoron: Ciaran Carson. A name obliged to two allegiances: Ciaran, from the Old Irish *ciar*, 'dark haired', hence 'little dark-haired one'; Carson, the name of the Dublin barrister whom many think to be the founder father of Northern Ireland. I was a kind of little dark horse. And years after that realisation, I would come to translate some of the work of the Cork poet Seán Ó Ríordáin (1916–1977), for whom Irish also lay in this twilight zone, referring to the things of home but not to those of the wider world: *an teanga seo leath-liom*, as he called it – 'this language half-mine', or, more accurately, 'this tongue half with me'. There is no Irish word for 'mine'. Nor, for that matter, is there a word for 'to have'. The closest to 'I have a horse' is *tá capall agam*, 'there is a horse at me'. Most interestingly, perhaps, Irish does not have words for 'yes' and 'no'. One responds to a question by using the verb employed in the question. For example, a possible answer to the question 'Is there a horse at you?' is 'There is'. Another, 'There is not'. And, of course, one can always evade the question altogether, and engage the questioner in some not entirely germane conversation. All this implies that different languages have different weights and measures, different sets of social and phenomenological expectations.

At any rate, Ó Ríordáin was preoccupied with the relationship of language to experience. In a long foreword to his first collection *Eireaball Spideoige* (*A Robin's Tail*), he argues that poetry is a form of prayer in which language strives to utter the nature of the things it signifies. He begins with a question: *Cad is filíocht ann?* – which one might translate as 'What is poetry?'; but in Irish, there's more to it than that, and one needs some circumlocution to get into its deep grammar – 'Where does poetry reside?', for example, or 'Poetry consists of what?'. Ó Ríordáin continues, as I translate his words:

> The mind of a child? Imagine two people in a room, a child and his father, and a horse going by on the street outside. The father looks out and says: 'There's Mary's horse going past.' That is a narration. It would seem the father loses the horse because he remains outside of it. Say a horse is a disease. The father doesn't catch that disease. The horse does not enrich the father's life. But the child – the child empathises with the sound of the horse. He savours the sound of the horse for the sake of the sound itself. And he listens to the sound grow dim – diminishing – until it recedes into silence. And he wonders at both sound and silence. As he discerns the rear legs of the horse he ponders their authority and their antiquity. And the world brims with horse-amazement and canter-magic. It's like – like having another countenance (under another appearance; hallucination). The child dwells in his encounter with the horse. And that, I think, is poetry.

We remember that the horse in 'Stopping by Woods' 'gives his harness bells a shake / To ask if there is some mistake'. The horse allows us another take on things, and I am reminded of the horse that features in a poem by Seán Ó Ríordáin:

Malairt

> Gaibh i leith, arsa Turnbull, go bhfeice tú an brón
> I súilibh an chapaill,
> Da mbeadh crúba chomh mór leo sin fútsa bheadh brón
> Id shúilibh chomh maith leis.
>
> Agus b'fhollas gur thuig sé chomh maith sin an brón
> I súilibh an chapaill,
> Is gur mhachnaigh chomh cruaidh air gur tomadh é fá dheoidh
> In aigne an chapaill.

D'fhéachas ar an gcapall go bhfeicinn an brón
　　'Na shúilibh ag seasamh,
Do chonac súile Turnbull ag féachaint im threo
　　As cloigeann an chapaill.

D'fhéachas ar Turnbull is d'fhéachas air fá dhó
　　Is do chonac ar a leacain
Na súile rómhóra bhí balbh le brón –
　　Súile an chapaill.

Swap (Double Take)

'Come over here,' said Turnbull, 'till you see the sorrow
　　In the horse's eyes.
If under you were hooves as cumbersome, there would
　　Be gloom in your eyes too.'

And it was plain to me, that he'd realised the sorrow
　　In the horse's eyes so well,
So deeply had he contemplated it, that he was steeped
　　Completely in the horse's mind.

I looked at the horse, that I might see the sorrow
　　Standing in its eyes,
And saw instead the eyes of Turnbull looking at me
　　From the horse's head.

I looked at Turnbull, then I took a second look,
　　And saw looming from his head
The too-big eyes that were dumb with sorrow –
　　The horse's eyes.

That poem, it seems to me, is at least partly about Ó Ríordáin's linguistic dilemma. As if the horse were the Irish language, and Turnbull his English alter ego. They are tied in a knot; they are obliged to each other, and are compelled to see the world through each other's eyes.

When I came to translate the *Inferno* of Dante, I came to realise that
it was riddled with such knots, such mutual metamorphoses. 'Knot'
in Italian is *nodo*, which can also mean a bond or an obligation, an
outcome. A node. There is an expression in Italian, *tutti i nodi
vengono al pettine*, 'all your combing will come to knots', or 'your sins
will find you out'. So it is in the *Inferno*, no more so than in Canto
XIII, in the Second Ring of the Seventh Circle of Hell, the Wood of
the Suicides. Here, the chancellor Piero delle Vigne, the sweet-
talking vine, has, for his sins, become a thorn tree. Virgil and
Dante are led to this circle by the centaur Nessus, who is half-man,
half-horse:

> Not yet had Nessus reached the other bank,
> > when we set foot within a sombre wood,
> > where, looking for a path, we drew a blank.
>
> Not green the leaves, for they are ashen-hued;
> > not smooth the boughs, but gnarled and full of knots;
> > not juicy fruit, but poisoned thorns extrude.
>
> Not half so rough or dense the habitats
> > of those wild beasts that shun the planted crests
> > between Corneto and Cecina's flats.
>
> Here the horrible Harpies make their nests,
> > who drove the Trojans from the Strophades
> > with doleful prophecies. Harpies are pests.
>
> Wide-winged, with human necks and faces, Harpies
> > are talon-toed and feather-bellied, and sit
> > uttering eerie cries in their eyrie trees . . .

Those lines, as I translated them, had a strangely familiar ring. It
took me a while to realise that John Boyle O'Reilly – who might or
might not have committed suicide – must also have been familiar
with them. For when, in Springfield, Mass., in the John Boyle
O'Reilly Club, I opened the book entitled *John Boyle O'Reilly: His*

Life, Poems and Speeches, my eye fell on these lines, from a long poem set in Australia, the country of his exile. This is what I read, years before I read the *Inferno* of Dante:

> In that strange country, whence comes the breath
> Of hot disease and pestilential death,
> Lie leagues of wooded swamp, that from the hills
> Seem stretching meadows; but the flood that fills
> Those valley-basins has the hue of ink,
> And dismal doorways open on the brink,
> Beneath the gnarlèd arms of trees that grow
> All leafless to the top, from roots below
> The Lethe flood; and he who enters there
> Beneath their screen sees rising, ghastly-bare,
> Like mammoth bones within a charnel dark,
> The white and ragged stems of paper-bark,
> That drip down moisture with a ceaseless drip,
> From lines that run like cordage of a ship;
> For myriad creepers struggle to the light,
> And twine and mat o'erhead in murderous fight
> For life and sunshine, like another race
> That wars on brethren for the highest place.
> Beneath the water and the matted screen,
> The baldhead vultures, two and two, are seen
> In dismal grandeur, with revolting face
> Of foul grotesque, like spirits of the place;
> And now and then a spear-shaped wave goes by,
> Its apex glittering with an evil eye
> That sets above its enemy and prey,
> As from the wave in treacherous, slimy way
> The black snake winds, and strikes the bestial bird,
> Whose shriek-like wailing on the hills is heard.

I remembered again my encounter with the spirit of Robert Frost, the day before I first stumbled into the work of John Boyle O'Reilly. *Whose woods these are I think I know.* Dante's *Inferno* famously begins in a wood: 'Halfway through the journey of our life / I found myself in a dark wood.' And the last circle of Hell, the furthest away from the light and heat of God, is a frozen lake. It is not a million miles away from Frost:

> My little horse must think it queer
> To stop without a farmhouse near
> Between the woods and frozen lake
> The darkest evening of the year.

Between the woods and frozen lake is precisely the territory of the *Inferno*, and it was only after reading Dante that I realised that Frost's rhyme scheme, aaba bbcb, and so on, is a skewed version of Dante's *terza rima*. Frost, when he was asked if 'On Stopping by Woods on a Snowy Evening' might be about suicide, replied that he didn't know, but that it was 'loaded with ulteriority'.

Ulteriority, and uncertainty. *Mi ritrovai per una selva oscura* – 'I came to in a dark wood'. That is the landscape in which poetry, and translations, are found. *Whose woods these are I think I know.* Recently, when I came to translate the '*Cúirt an Mheán Oíche*' – 'The Midnight Court' – of Brian Merriman, I realised that Merriman, too, must have known Dante. 'The Midnight Court' is an *aisling*, a dream vision; so is the *Inferno*. Merriman's poem happens in a space which is not quite of this world; yet it deals with the realities of this world. Briefly, it is a tirade by the women of Ireland against the inadequate sexuality of Irish men; it is a yearning for an ideal world, in which both women and men can find joyful expression in their being, and Ireland is free from the chains of bad law.

In Merriman's *aisling*, his fairy woman is not beautiful, but a threatening monster. The vision that she discloses veers between a possible paradise, and the present reality. Merriman's poem, for all its rhetorical and satirical extravagance, gives us a real sense of what life must have been like in eighteenth-century Ireland: its people and their speech, their gestures, their dress, their food and drink, their recreations, and, of course, their sexual mores. The atmosphere of the 'Court' is not so much that of a court of law but of a country market, filled with verbal commotion and colour. For all that, it is still a dream-world, where Merriman can free himself from the restraints of conventional discourse, swooping from high rhetoric to street-talk in the space of a few lines – much as Dante did in the *Inferno*. And language is very much a concern of the *aisling*: a recurrent theme is the poet's lament for the decline of Irish and its support mechanism of noble patronage.

I am not qualified to write about the linguistic demographics of eighteenth-century Ireland, but the Irish language in Clare must have been on the wane even then. Merriman's language is driven towards its maximum potential, or into excess, by the fury of its protagonists. Its sometimes desperate rhetoric is always done with immense panache. Even when it lapses into logorrhoea, it questions itself. Often, Merriman, not content to say a thing once, must say it six or seven times. A classic example is the couplet, towards the end of the poem, where he plays on his own name:

> *Is taibhseach taitneamhach tairbheach tréitheach*
> *Meidhreach meanmach a ainm 's is aerach.*

Which means something like 'Spirited pleasant useful versatile merry mindful and lively his name'; but the effect, of near-homophones collapsing into one another, of meanings slithering into one another, is untranslatable. Let's take one word, *aerach*, which can indeed mean 'lively' or 'fond of pleasure'; but *aerach* is also 'airy', not only in the sense of 'carefree' but of 'volatile', and in Merriman's hands the language is indeed volatile, as its essence is pressurised, letting off steam, ever threatening to boil and vanish into thin air through its own excesses. However, the couplet is spoken not by the 'Merriman' narrator, but by the Young Woman, in a voice of contemptuous irony, so that it comes to mean the opposite of what it says. For *aerach* can also mean 'flighty', 'improvident', 'vain'. Things depend on how you say them, and who is doing the saying, and who the listening. The words, the more that you look at them, become foreign, eerie and strange: and *aerach* also means 'haunted', or 'weird'. Dinneen's Irish–English dictionary has the expression *áit aerach*, 'a lonely place, a place haunted by ghosts', which is the landscape in which the poem itself is set; and then we realise that the first word in the couplet, *taibhseach*, does indeed mean 'spirited'; but it also means 'ghostly'. For the protagonists of the 'Court', including 'Merriman' himself, are ghosts, summoned into being by language; they are figments of the imagination. In the 'Court' the language itself is continually interrogated, and Merriman is the great illusionist, continually spiriting words into another dimension. The language is loaded with ulteriority.

What is a translator to do with all this? As soon as I began to deal with Merriman, I knew that my own grasp of Irish was not up to his manifold command. I hesitate to call myself a native speaker: true, Irish is, or was, my first language, but I learned it from parents for whom it was a second language; and it has not been the first language in which I think, or express myself, for a long time, though I sometimes dream in it. Compared with my English, my Irish is impoverished. Yet I can remember a time when English was foreign to me: a time when my father would tell me stories of the Fianna and other heroes of ancient Ireland. I remember the landscape in which they were set; and, as I worked my way through the translation, it sometimes seemed to me that I entered that otherworld where it is always nightfall: I have been hunting, but have got separated from my companions, and I make my way through a dark wood before emerging into a mountainy region where a few lights glimmer on the hillside. These are the houses where the word-hoards are concealed. Sometimes I would work past midnight, or lie sleepless in bed, haunted by an elusive phrase. *And miles to go before I sleep.* I would get up and scribble the words down; often, when I looked at them in the morning they would crumble into dust, like jewels brought back from an enchanted realm, which cannot bear the light of this world. Marcel Proust says somewhere that a writer inhabits his native language as if it were a foreign country. For me, both languages – so familiar yet so foreign – became strange as I wandered the borders between them. I realised my inadequacy in both. Trying to find English equivalents for Merriman's abundant lexicon of vilification, for his numerous double entendres, for the gorgeousness of his verbal music, I scoured thesauruses and dictionaries. I racked my brains. *And miles to go before I sleep.* Eventually I got there.

I was helped on my journey by a reference in John O'Daly's *Poets and Poetry of Munster* (1860) to Merriman's having been 'a wild youth and fond of amusement, a taste which he acquired from being an excellent performer on the violin'. It prompted me to think of him as a precursor of the great Clare fiddle masters whose music I had first encountered in the 1970s – the likes of Junior Crehan, John Kelly, Bobby Casey, P.J. Hayes, Patrick Kelly of Cree, Paddy Canny, and Martin Rochford of Bodyke, a few miles from Feakle; men of great subtle wit and intelligence, full of verbal as well as musical dexterity, who could not only play, but sing songs, recite recitations, dance, tell stories and lies – 'lies' being tall tales or elaborate 'wind-ups', presented with the appearance of truth, very much in the tradition of 'The Midnight Court'. And as I read '*Cúirt an Mheán Oíche*', I was struck that the whole thing might be recited, or sung, to the measure of an Irish jig:

> 'Twas my custom to stroll by a clear winding stream,
> With my boots full of dew from the lush meadows green,
> Near a neck of the woods where the mountain holds sway,
> Without danger or fear at the dawn of the day.
> The sight of Lough Graney would dazzle my eyes,
> As the countryside sparkled beneath the blue skies,
> Uplifting the mountains, arranged stack upon stack,
> Each head peeping over a neighbouring back.
> It would lighten the heart, be it listless with age,
> Enfeebled by folly, or cardiac rage –
> Your wherewithal racked by financial disease –
> To perceive through a gap in the wood full of trees
> A squadron of ducks in a shimmering bay,
> Escorting the swan on her elegant way,
> The trout on the rise with its mouth to the light,
> While the perch swims below like a speckledy sprite,
> And the billows of blue become foam as they break
> With a thunderous crash on the shores of the lake,
> And the birds in the trees whistle bird-songs galore,
> The deer gallop lightly though woods dark as yore,
> Where trumpeting huntsmen and hounds of the hunt
> Chase the shadow of Reynard, who leads from the front . . .

On the morning of New Year's Day, 2005 – the year of the two-hundredth anniversary of Merriman's death – I dreamed about Merriman. I was wandering on a dark hillside when I saw a light in the distance. I followed it, and came to a little house. The door was ajar; timidly, I pushed it open. Merriman was sitting by the hearth, wearing a greatcoat. I suspected he might have had a fiddle concealed in its folds. He gestured at me to sit down. I did so, and we conversed. True, he did most of the talking, but I was fully able to follow the flow of his intricate Irish. I cannot remember what was said. When I awoke, I was disappointed to find my Irish restored to its former poverty. But I felt that my English had been enriched by that encounter: one which a year ago would have been impossible, for the thought of translating Merriman had never entered my mind until I was commissioned to do so by Cumann Merriman, the Merriman Society – just as I had never dreamed of approaching Dante until I was commissioned, by Jamie McKendrick, the poet and distinguished translator of Italian poetry, to translate a canto of the *Inferno*. I would never have taken those roads had someone else not taken them for me. I would not be standing here delivering this particular lecture had I not been prompted to recite 'On Stopping by Woods on a Snowy Evening' many years ago in Amherst, Massachusetts. 'Way leads on to way', as Robert Frost has it in 'The Road Not Taken'. The genesis of that poem might lie in a letter written by him to Susan Hayes Howard on 10 February 1912:[2]

> Two lonely cross-roads that themselves cross each other I have walked several times this winter without meeting or overtaking so much as a single person on foot or on runners. The practically unbroken condition of both for several days after a snow or a blow proves that neither is much travelled. Judge then how surprised I was the other evening as I came down one to see a man, who to my own unfamiliar eyes and in the dusk looked for all the world like myself, coming down the other, his approach to the point where our paths must intersect being so timed that unless one of us pulled up we must inevitably collide. I felt as if I was going to meet my own image in a slanting mirror. Or say I felt as we slowly converged on the same point with the same noiseless yet laborious stride as if we were two

images about to float together with the uncrossing of someone's eyes. I verily expected to take up or absorb this other self and feel the stronger by the addition for the three-mile journey home. But I didn't go forward to the touch. I stood still in wonderment and let him pass by; and that, too, with the fatal omission of not trying to find out by a comparison of lives and immediate and remote interests what could have brought us by crossing paths to the same point in a wilderness at the same moment of nightfall. Some purpose I doubt not, if we could but have made it out. I like a coincidence almost as well as an incongruity.

If my wanderings between Irish and English and the Italian of Dante have been as incongruous as they are coincidental, so be it. Poetry – and translation – reside in that ambiguity. *Whose woods these are I think I know?*

1   In Robert Welch's *The Oxford Companion to Irish Literature* (1996), the *aisling* is defined as 'a Gaelic literary genre, primarily associated with the political poetry of the eighteenth century, though having roots in early Irish literary texts dealing both with love and sovereignty'. Typically, 'the poet wanders forth and meets a fairy woman who is described in terms of traditional and conventional formulas; he engages in dialogue with her and asks her name, and she identifies herself as Ireland, forsaken by her legitimate spouse. The aisling ends with the woman declaiming a prophecy of the return of the rightful Stuart king.'

2   See Elizabeth Shepley Sergeant, *Robert Frost: The Trial by Existence* (Harcourt, 1960).

Notes on Contributors

GARY ALLEN was born in Ballymena, County Antrim. His poetry has been published widely in magazines including *The Honest Ulsterman*, *Metre*, *Cyphers*, *Agenda* and *Stand*. He has published three collections of poetry: *Languages* (Flambard/Black Mountain, 2002), *Exile* (Black Mountain, 2004) and *North of Nowhere* (Lagan Press, 2006); and one novel, *Cillin* (Black Mountain, 2006).

SUSAN ASHE, who was born in India and lives in Hampshire, is at work on a second novel and a collection of stories. She has published numerous literary translations and is also the author of two children's books, *Cuda of the Celts* (Egmont, 2003) and *Fillet and the Mob* (Egmont, 2004).

CIARAN CARSON is Professor of Poetry and Director of the Seamus Heaney Centre for Poetry at Queen's University Belfast. His translation of the Old Irish epic *Táin Bó Cuailnge* (*The Táin*) will be published by Penguin Classics in 2007.

PETER N. DALE was born in Melbourne, Australia. He is the author of *The Myth of Japanese Uniqueness* (Croom Helm, 1986). He moved to Italy in the early 1980s and his interest in dialect poetry there stimulated him to translate and annotate the entire body of sonnets written in Roman dialect by Guiseppe Gioachino Belli. He currently lives in Palestrina, Italy.

PAUL FARLEY has published three collections of poetry, and his most recent, *Tramp in Flames* (Picador), is a Poetry Book Society Recommendation for Autumn 2006. He has received numerous awards, including the Somerset Maugham Award and the Whitbread Poetry Award. He currently holds a Readership in Poetry at Lancaster University.

MICHAEL FOLEY was born in Derry, and lives in London where he lectures in Information Technology at the University of Westminster. His fourth collection of poetry, *Autumn Beguiles the Fatalist*, was published by Blackstaff Press in 2006. He has also published four novels and a collection of translations of French poetry.

ALAN GILLIS lectures in English at Edinburgh University. He is the author of *Irish Poetry of the 1930s* (Oxford University Press, 2005). His first collection of poetry, *Somebody, Somewhere* (Gallery Press, 2004), was shortlisted for the *Irish Times* Poetry Now Award and won the 2005 Rupert and Eithne Strong Award.

SEÁN LYSAGHT grew up in Limerick and lives in Westport, County Mayo. He is the author of *Robert Lloyd Praeger: The Life of a Naturalist* (Four Courts, 1998) and of four collections of poetry, of which the most recent was *Erris* (Gallery Press, 2002).

NIALL McGRATH is the editor of *The Black Mountain Review*. He is the author of a verse drama, a novel and several pamphlets and collections of poetry, the most recent of which is *Reversion* (Black Mountain, 2003). He is a tutor for the Open College of the Arts.

PATRICK McGUINNESS was born in Tunisia, and is a Fellow of St Anne's College, Oxford, where he lectures in French. He lives in Caernarfon, Wales. His collection of poems, *The Canals of Mars* (2005) and translation of Stéphane Mallarmé's *For Anatole's Tomb* (2003) are published by Carcanet.

DEREK MAHON was born in Belfast and lives in Kinsale, County Cork. His collection *Harbour Lights* (Gallery Press, 2005) won the 2006 *Irish Times* Poetry Now Award. The poems here are from *Adaptations*, also published by Gallery Press in 2006.

MARY O'DONNELL is a poet, fiction-writer and broadcaster based in County Kildare. She has presented several series of poetry programmes for RTÉ radio, most recently *Crossing the Lines*, on European poetry in translation. *The Place of Miracles: New and Selected Poems* is published in 2006 by New Island Books.

FRANCIS O'HARE is a teacher living in Belfast. His poems have been published in *The Honest Ulsterman*, *Fortnight*, and the *Irish News*, among others. A selection was included in *Poetry Introductions 1* (Lagan Press, 2005).

DON PATERSON lives in Kirriemuir, Angus. His most recent collection of poems, *Landing Light*, won the T.S. Eliot Prize and the Whitbread Poetry Award. His version of Rilke's *Sonnets to Orpheus* was published by Faber in October 2006. He teaches at St Andrew's University.

We are grateful to Picador for allowing us to publish five poems by Paul Farley from *Tramp in Flames* (2006); to Faber & Faber for three poems by Don Paterson from *Orpheus* (2006); and to Gallery Press for three poems by Derek Mahon from *Adaptations* (2006).